Of Time and Widowhood

Of Time and Widowhood

Nationwide Studies of Enduring Effects

Herbert H. Hyman

Duke Press Policy Studies

Durham, N.C.   1983

Library of Congress Cataloging in Publication Data

Hyman, Herbert Hiram, 1918–
   Of time and widowhood.

   (Duke Press policy studies)
   Bibliography: p.
   Includes index.
   1. Widows—United States—Longitudinal studies.
2. Widowers—United States—Longitudinal studies.
3. Family life surveys—United States. 4. Family—
United States. I. Title. II. Series
HQ1058.5.U5H95 1983   306.8′8   82–25138
ISBN 0–8223–0504–6

In memory of my widowed mother

Contents

Tables

Acknowledgments

A grant from the National Institute of Mental Health enabled me to conduct these studies, and a period as scholar-in-residence at the Rockefeller Foundation's Study Center in Bellagio, Italy, enabled me to complete the writing of this monograph. I express my appreciation to both foundations for their generosity. The survey data that served as the source materials were obtained from the Inter-University Consortium for Political and Social Research and the National Opinion Research Center, for which I thank them. For their fine work in programming and processing those data, I also thank Janet Morgan and James Dray of Wesleyan University, and for special tabulation of attrition in the panel data, I thank Maria Sanchez of the University of Michigan. For consultation on various technical matters, I am grateful to Richard Boyd and Robert Rosenbaum. For many good suggestions throughout the analysis and for careful review of the manuscript, I owe a special debt to Charles R. Wright. For valuable criticism and encouragement I give special thanks to Matilda and John Riley. Once again, I thank Irene Spinnler for her help in the course of the work and for her careful typing of the manuscript. My wife's help, and her tolerance toward and encouragement of work on so painful a theme, deserves special appreciation.

Acknowledgments

Of Time and Widowhood

1. Old and New Avenues to Knowledge of the Effects of Widowhood

Widowhood is one of the sad facts of life millions of men and women learn firsthand only in their later years. Indeed, for those fortunate enough to live long it is ironic but inevitable—except in the rarest of instances—that they must experience the misfortune of widowhood, and then generally carry its burdens for many more years. Those burdens must be borne while they are old, at the stage in life when they may be poorer, sicker, more dependent, and likely to have developed deep attachments to the spouses they have lost. Among those so unfortunate as to be widowed at an early age, most have the special burden of rearing and supporting young children by themselves. And whether old or young, women bear the burden disproportionately—the ratio of widows to widowers in the United States in the mid-1970s being around 5:1—and must carry it along with the other disadvantages society has imposed.

Given the numbers involved and the possible severity of the social problems of widowhood, one would expect to find applied research, large in scale and fine in quality, that would enrich our knowledge of its social and psychological effects and guide our efforts to evaluate and ameliorate the burdens. One would also expect to find basic research of the scale and quality warranted by the fundamental nature of the experiences involved in widowhood. Those experiences penetrate the very heart of the individual. They shatter the family, that central institution of society. If ever there were a variable that tested the vitality of the individual and the strength of the social fabric, widowhood is it. Such extremely powerful variables, however cold and calculating the strategy may seem, are especially attractive to investigators acute enough to sense the extra-special yield from such research. Thus they have studied the social-psychological impact of a flood that inundated a community in West Virginia, of a coal mine disaster on a town in Nova Scotia, of the bombings of cities in World War II and the forced evacuation of the young children, of the prolonged unemployment of almost every worker in a factory town in Austria during the Great Depression. Oddly enough, such powerful, but remote and fortunately rare events have been studied more rigorously and continuously than widowhood which happens to multitudes around us all the time, is more accessible for elaborate study, and which should command the sympathies and best efforts of basic researchers.

That widowhood can create severe problems is painfully obvious. Consider this report from a widow in Chicago.

I wanted to take my life, end it all. It was a Saturday morning two weeks ago. I got up, I was so depressed. If I'd had sleeping pills I would have taken them, cause I was so low. I felt "what's the sense of me waking up? What's there for me to wake up to?" That's the day I called up my niece long distance and I told her. I told her how depressed I was. She asked "Is there anyone there to give you sleeping pills?" I said "no." She said "If you have any, throw them in the toilet." I didn't have any. . . . I still feel that way. Several times I think "What's the use? What's there to live for?" It's two weeks since I felt that way. I can eat very little. I saw a doctor a month ago. He didn't pinpoint it. He wants to put me in the hospital but I can't go because Medicare won't pay for one year (Lopata, 1979:361).

A widow in Boston is an equally sad case.

"It doesn't seem to be much better," said Mrs. H., 13 months after her bereavement. She was still irritable, lonely, and insecure, easily tired and depressed. "I could never feel like myself again," she said. She had tried to avoid thinking about her husband throughout the year but memories would break through despite her attempts to avoid them and then she would feel very frightened. "Sometimes I wake up in the morning . . . and I see him. You know I see his face, or a gesture he might have made, or in the casket, and then I get very unnerved and I just get up and start doing something. There's no other way (sobbing), it isn't any better—no better than it ever will be" (Parkes, 1975: 133).

An old widower in the South had a similar trauma: "I'm just as lonely for my wife today as I was the day she passed away, seven years ago. I went to pieces then and I still can't forget her. I don't believe in suicide or I would have done it" (Cosneck, 1970: 372).

After reading such documented cases, no one should doubt that widowhood can create severe problems, but one should still question the scale of severity. How common are these cases? How long do such problems usually last? Reliable and generalizable answers are essential to guide our sympathies toward sensible solutions and sound social policies.

Surprisingly, past studies of widowhood do not provide the answers. They have been based on small, sometimes biased samples of restricted, occasionally peculiar, populations. The difficulties in drawing generalizable conclusions are compounded by the narrow domain of effects examined, the short timespan within which the effects are traced, and the specific historical period when the widowed have been studied. And often the validity of the conclusions is doubtful because of inadequacies in the research design and deficiencies in the measurement of the effects. Some readers may not be surprised by this catalogue of criticisms. The source of such difficulties seems obvious to them: the meager money, manpower, and time allotted to past research. The future remedy also seems simple to them: provide lavish resources. That remedy is neither simple nor satisfactory. Resources, however lavish, are never adequate; the supply cannot keep up with the demand. Large-scale studies of widowhood that follow the conventional path of the past would be not only exceedingly costly, but would still suffer some of the limitations inherent in the old approaches to the problem.

We have taken a new, almost completely neglected path to knowledge of the social and psychological effects of widowhood. The secondary analysis of sample surveys—the extraction of findings on problems different from those that were the primary concern of surveys already completed and now available for public use—provides the avenue to obtain substantial evidence on the problem. We selected nine nationwide surveys conducted by two agencies noted for the quality of their sampling and measurement procedures, the first survey dating from 1956 and the last from 1978. All were chosen because they have relevant content, identify the widowed and nonwidowed in the samples and measure their other important characteristics, and have special technical features appropriate for the study. Thus, in ways we shall describe in detail later, they yield replicated generalizable evidence on a variety of effects of widowhood based on comparisons of large numbers of widowed and nonwidowed individuals representative of these contrasted groups all across the nation.

All this evidence was obtained quickly and economically since the surveys were already completed and the heavy investment of time, money, and manpower had already been sustained by the agencies and their original sponsors. Indeed we would have had to be as rich as Rockefeller and as patient as Job to have carried out these nine elegant national surveys between 1956 and 1978. Via secondary analysis we reaped the rewards from earlier heavy investors. Other investigators can follow this new path, replicating our tests, expanding the statistical base, and, by judicious selection from the wealth of available surveys, enlarging the domain to be explored for possible effects of widowhood. With a tiny investment, they, too, can earn a profitable yield.

Old Studies and New Guidelines

Before marking the specific steps we took along the new path, let us examine selected examples of the four major types of past studies. By documenting their weaknesses, strengths, and some crucial findings, we can present the guidelines for sound study of the effects of widowhood which we tried to follow.

Studies of Patients

Take as the prototype for one class of studies Parkes' early investigations of grief following the death of a family member (1965: Parts 1 & 2). The base for conclusions about the effects of widowhood was nine relatively young, recently widowed patients (seven were widows) in psychiatric treatment at the clinics of two London hospitals in the years 1958–60. Ignore the narrow target population, young, recently widowed Londoners in the late 1950s, to which the conclusions, at best, would refer. Ignore the small size of the sample. Those limitations weaken any generalizations, but much worse is the biased method of sampling. Parkes had only a self-selected sample from that population: those who had become so sad and so sick within six months of the bereavement that they entered treatment. Others—some sick but some healthy, and the "merry widows"—who did not need or want treatment were not sampled.

There are three other more subtle biases which as critical and sophisticated an investigator as Parkes notes. He only sampled certain kinds of hospitals. He found few psychosomatic disorders among the widowed but he stresses, "Since patients are seldom referred [to those two hospitals]—for treatment of psychosomatic conditions it is not surprising that few cases were found in the present study" (Part 2: 21). From within the special patient population of those special hospitals, the final sample of the bereaved then arrived at Parkes' door via referrals from other psychiatrists on the staff who had been alerted to his special interest. "It seems likely, therefore, that patients whose illness was most clearly related to their bereavement were more often brought to the attention of the writer than patients whose illness was only incidental" (Part 1: 3–4). Then still a third source of sampling bias was introduced by a procedure that characterizes almost all studies, no matter what the sampling design, and which deserves special note. Of those "who were brought to the notice of the investigators . . . six . . . were not included because they refused . . . to give a detailed account of their reaction to the bereavement" (Part I: 2). For these many reasons, generalizations by Parkes and others who conducted similar studies, even to the narrow target populations are risky and, of course, cannot be extended beyond the boundaries of those populations.[1]

The classic papers by Parkes sensitize one to many methodological problems of research design and measurement, as well as sampling. Those most suggestive for our guidelines deserve special, if brief, note. In addition to the nine widowed patients, Parkes interviewed twelve other bereaved patients from the two clinics who had lost a parent, sibling, or child. What is immediately suggested is the possibility of establishing effects that are distinctive to the bereavement of widowhood and those common to many or all forms of bereavement. The inclusion of various comparison or "control" groups along with the widowed would provide the evidence. This promising design seems to have been completely neglected by all investigators, including Parkes himself who makes no use of this comparison implicit in his design.

Oddly enough, the conventional control group, patients who have experienced no bereavement of any kind, is almost never included in such studies, even though Parkes stresses its crucial importance in establishing whether the phenomena observed are equally common among the nonbereaved and thus not effects of widowhood. In describing the symptoms reported by Marris in a study of widows to be reviewed below, Parkes remarks: "All were common symptoms . . . and it seems likely that . . . most of them would be found in any series of middle-aged women." In discussing the incidence of various disorders among the bereaved reported by other investigators, Parkes underscores the point: "While the figures given . . . do suggest that these conditions may be caused by bereavement, in the absence of controls no definite conclusion can be drawn" (Part 2: 20).

Finally, two features of the measurement procedure suggest guidelines. All twenty-one patients were interviewed by Parkes. However skillful a psychiatrist he was, the procedure nevertheless puts us at the mercy of a single interviewer, moreover one who knew before he asked his first question that all the respondents had developed "symptoms during the terminal illness or within six months after the death of a parent, spouse, sibling, or child" (Part 1: 2).[2] The contrast with the procedures of our study and the implications for response bias will become clear later.

Studies of the Widowed Sampled from Death Records

A second class of studies in the literature uses a larger number of widowed cases drawn from official death records of some area, a rigorous and unbiased method of sampling. For example, Marris (1958) drew from such records the names of 100 young (mean age forty-two) widows living in three working class areas of London, shortly after their bereavement in the early 1950s. Similarly Parkes, transplanted to the United States along with Glick and Weiss, drew a sample of 349 widows and widowers under the age of forty-five, living in the Boston area shortly after their bereavement in 1965–66, limiting it to those whose death records indicated natural causes or accident (1974, 1975). Perhaps the most exotic example of such studies is by Danto (1975) who drew a sample of widows of Detroit police officers, slain on duty, from the records of the department. Ingenious and informative as this study may be, it hardly sheds light on the condition of widows generally. Confining such samples to those recently bereaved within one area has the logistical and economic advantage that the addresses are likely to be up-to-date, few respondents will have to be traced and interviewed in new and remote locations, and the field work is simplified. Restricting the sample to the young, recently bereaved has the added advantage for investigators that effects are captured at a peak point, before they are dissipated with time in an especially vulnerable group, since, as Parkes remarks, "other studies had shown that the untimely death of a husband or wife gives rise to a more severe . . . reaction . . . than in old age" (1975: 120).

Such benefits exact a price. The generalizations must be qualified in terms of the age of the population and the recency of the widowhood, the class and cultural composition of the area, and the social service provisions of the place and time period. Granted that the study of short-term effects among the young is important and provides a maximum estimate of the effects of widowhood, this cannot deny the importance of studying long-term effects among the old and the young, and establishing the complete range or average level of effects. In theory, of course, the design could be used for broader, larger, longer, unbiased study of the effects of widowhood but it has not been applied that way in practice, and perhaps never can be because of inherent, intractable problems.[3]

Ethical investigators, following the canons of informed consent, always begin such studies by writing and/or telephoning or visiting the respondents or using an intermediary to inform them that they wish to discuss their bereavement. "Unwillingness to review painful memories" causes many to refuse (Glick, Weiss, and Parkes, 1974: 22). Compassionate investigators are "intensely aware of the assault that fate had visited on the people we hoped to recruit into our study." Understandably and properly they decide to "forego the usual pressures used by survey studies to assure themselves of an adequate response rate. . . . We would not attempt to convince the initially reluctant that they should nevertheless participate" (1974: 21). The net result of such refusals on top of the usual losses from changes of address, not-at-homes, etc. is that Marris' 100 cases dwindled to 72; Glick, Weiss, and Parkes' 349 shrunk to 68; Danto ended up with 10 police widows. The investigators then must face the murky question of evaluating the bias from the loss of those so badly affected that they cannot talk about their bereavement and the inclusion of those so affected that they seize the opportunity to talk about it. That task calls for technical virtuosity, may be shirked, and may be insuperable.[4]

The compassionate approach and the virtuosity required in reducing and then estimating the residual bias from refusals is best illustrated in a study in St. Louis by Clayton, Halikas, and Maurice (1972). They used newspaper obituaries as an initial sampling frame which resulted in a very low rate of consent to be interviewed. Then by switching to official death records, they not only had an unbiased sampling frame, but also acquired the name of a clergyman. Whenever possible, he then acted as their intermediary to gain consent for an interview. Nevertheless, only 64 percent of such contacts resulted in interviews. The final sample from both sources shrunk to 109 cases. Attempts to estimate the bias through follow-up interviews with refusers and subsequent letters to them containing a brief instrument only resulted in more refusals. Finally, to estimate bias they compared the mortality of those bereaved who had refused and those who had been interviewed by checking the death records the following year.[5]

The thoughtful, most considerate way this design is always operated has another subtle, but important consequence. The respondents have been informed from the start that they are cast in the role of the widowed, one might say asked to *perform* that role, and obviously the interviewers also cannot help but know that scenario from the start. The danger of response error looms in this class of studies as it did in the first class, but we shall postpone this discussion until we review a third class of studies. It should be stressed, however, that the danger seems unavoidable given the canon of informed consent.

Studies of this type do not seem to incorporate control groups as an integral part of the research design, perhaps because of the extra cost involved in the field work. The control group of nonbereaved individuals obviously cannot be drawn from the death records. So another sampling frame or source for that group of cases has to be found elsewhere, involving extra labor and expense and the difficulty of drawing an unbiased sample of nonbereaved that is equivalent to or matched in some appropriate ways with the bereaved. Marris, for example, juxtaposed findings from Townsend's study of old people, done in London at the same time, which had included both the nonwidowed and the widowed (1957). Thus Marris obtained data from a control group at no cost. And he also could compare the old widows in Townsend's study with the young widows in his own study.

Strict comparability in the procedures and coverage of the two studies, however, is lacking because the two pieces are, so to speak, patched together, and not parts of one integral design. Glick, Weiss, and Parkes obtained a control group, from sources not clearly indicated, of sixty-eight married individuals matched on a profile of characteristics with their sixty-eight widowed cases.[6] Although Danto had an ideal source for a control group, the personnel records of the Detroit Police Department from which he could have drawn a rigorous sample of women whose policemen husbands had not died, he used no control group at all. In the absence of a control group in this or the other classes of studies, conclusions that the patterns observed are effects of widowhood may be false. At best, the investigator has what we have called a *pseudocomparative* research design, one in which he uses his imagination or general fund of knowledge to fill in the findings for the cell that is in fact missing in the design. If he had a truly comparative design, he might learn that his imagination had led him astray.

Localized Sample Surveys of the Widowed

A third and different class of studies are based on conventional sample surveys which, in contrast with secondary analysis, are especially conducted for the primary purpose of studying the effects of widowhood.

For example, Lopata (1971) commissioned the National Opinion Research Center to survey a sample of 301 widows—rigorously drawn from the population of metropolitan Chicago. As a result the sample was heterogeneous, including young and old widows, black and white, bereaved recently or long ago, poorer and better off. She was able to generalize and also establish by internal analysis the differential effects in subgroups of widows. (The substantial differences she found clearly indicate that other studies based on restricted, homogeneous populations of widows cannot be safely generalized.) Nevertheless, as a conservative investigator she also must limit her generalizations to metropolitan Chicago and the circumstances of widows when surveyed there in the late 1960s. Those generalizations were stretched a bit by juxtaposing findings from surveys of widows in other areas. So Lopata made good use of findings from surveys of small-town Missouri and Washington State, but such expedients of a resourceful, but not rich investigator, only stretched that far. Her high quality survey, even when limited to 301 widows in Chicago was a costly undertaking, and the lack of a control group and larger number of widows from more areas within the inquiry must stem, at least in part, from limited funds.

The point is underscored by Pihlblad and Adams' survey of a rigorously drawn sample of 849 widowed individuals, age sixty-five or older (698 were widows) and of a control group of elderly married men and women (1972).[7] This large and fine, no doubt costly survey containing a control group permits generalizations and valid conclusions, but these are limited to the universe covered: the elderly in small-town Missouri.

In a passing remark, Lopata tells us that "*All* our respondents *know that they should* feel grief and express it in mourning behavior" (1975: 49, italics supplied). We should not let it pass us by for it is full of import for the problems of measurement error and for our guidelines. It is hard to think of a social role more bound by custom, more strictly prescribed than that of the widowed. Although Lopata goes on to say that "Modern American society has been phasing out the *status role* of 'widow,' with its all-pervasive identity and its main function of maintaining the distinctions between a woman so labeled" and other women (1975: 47), it is still operative, as shown by her other remark and her findings.

The role prescription is a major social determinant of the effects of widowhood but it is also a source of measurement error in the three classes of studies, all of which in the very nature of their procedures label their respondents "widowed" and make that status salient. Lopata's remark might be amplified. All the respondents know how they should answer certain questions, and all the interviewers (they have read the label "widow") have expectations about the answers the respondents are likely to give. Admittedly, in primary surveys of the widowed, this source of error is not rampant since the content of many questions has no obvious relation to the role prescription, and unexpected effects of widowhood only become revealed through the later statistical analysis. In the other classes of studies that determine effects from a narrative account of the experience of widowhood, thus emphasizing the role continually, the value of the rich findings may be offset by the maximizing of this source of error. It is hard to see how any of the three methods can be made invulnerable to such error since the labeling for both interviewers and respondents is unavoidable. The structure of inquiry almost demands certain kinds of answers from the respondents, and the reinforced expectations of the interviewer also create real dangers, as shown by the methodological literature.[8]

As the reader can sense, secondary analysis of sample surveys is not vulnerable to this source of error. The surveys one exploits were not conducted for the purpose of studying widowhood, and correspondingly the inquiry was not presented in that light either to the respondents or the interviewers. The role of the widowed is never made salient. Indeed the routine question on marital status is normally buried in the midst of other background questions on age, occupation, religion, etc., and usually asked far along in the sequence of questions or at the tail end of a survey. To make the methodological distinction, our approach involves a double-blind design; the three classes of studies already reviewed have no blinds at all. This is not to deny that those studies can penetrate more deeply and directly into the nature of the experience.

Localized Sample Surveys of the Aged

Before describing our study, a fourth and final class of studies in the literature located at the point where the old path ends and the new path begins, will now be reviewed. Interest in the problems of the aged has led over the years to a series of surveys of well-designed samples of older individuals commissioned specifically to enlarge our knowledge of their problems. Since widowhood is such a common, one might say obvious, accompaniment of age, the investigators sometimes compare the older widowed individuals with a control group of older married individuals, both representative groups falling naturally into the sample in substantial numbers. Given the adequate numbers, subgroups representing various types of widowed can and have been examined.

When one considers the close and obvious connection between age and widowhood, it is surprising to learn that such analyses frequently are neglected. Indeed the two variables often remain confounded, and findings reported as effects of old age often reflect the buried effects of widowhood. (By the same token, the effects of widowhood in any such analyses cannot be inferred unless age is controlled.) One soon realizes that the analyst's vision, given the immediate, explicit purpose of the survey, is narrowed down to the aged, and he does not see what is right before his eyes: the riches available to him for the study of widowhood. Berardo, a most knowledgeable investigator and bibliographer of the field remarks:

> One apparent and somewhat paradoxical reason for the dearth of information in this area is that, in recent efforts to give needed attention to the later stages of the life-cycle, social scientists have tended to submerge the identifications of the widowed through their concentration on the problems of our aged population. Specifically, data on the aged often are not distinguished with respect to widowhood status (1968: 199).

Fortunately, what surveyors of the aged have ignored need not be lost forever. It can be exploited by secondary analysis. Berardo is a case in point (1967). Ten years after a 1956 survey of the aged had been conducted in Thurston County, Washington, he extracted from it groups of 181 aged widows, 44 widowers, and a control group of 271 aged married individuals. From his many substantive findings only one, specifically relevant to our study, will be noted. Widowers and widows showed different adaptations to their situation, the effects of widowhood in some spheres being more traumatic for men. His findings, of course, cannot be generalized beyond the special context of the timing of the original survey, the rural character and location of the county, and the age of the population (sixty-five or older) that was sampled.

Two other complementary examples of this class of studies illustrate the benefits, but also the limitations. Kutner et al. surveyed a large, well-designed sample of the aged in the Yorkville district of New York City in 1952, and isolated for special analysis a group of 220 widowed individuals. These were subdivided by the length of widowhood, and when compared with each other and with the married in the sample established the effects of widowhood. Married women had higher "morale" than "those widowed ten years or less. However no significant differences in morale appear between the women widowed ten years or more and those who are married" (1960: 64).[9] Similarly, Townsend surveyed a good sample of the aged in a working class district of London in the 1950s. His comparisons of nonwidowed and widowed subgroups divided by length of widowhood once again established that effects were more marked among those recently widowed. He also found differential effects for widows and widowers, greater effects being observed among the men.[10] The consistent findings of the two studies caution us against overgeneralizing from studies exclusively of those recently bereaved. These two, taken together, provide a replication and a cross-national test, but the conclusions are still limited to the aged, the specific social conditions of the districts sampled, and the historical context of the 1950s.

Sample surveys of the aged that are nationwide are very scarce. Two that are available illustrate the potential in this class of studies, and also show vividly the neglect of the variable of widowhood in such primary analyses. In 1974 the Louis Harris agency surveyed a nationwide sample of about 3,000 individuals aged sixty-five or older, as well as a sample of the general population with an over-sampling of those aged fifty-five to sixty-five, and in 1981 conducted an equivalent survey to examine trends and explore new areas. Such relevant variables as life satisfaction, self-image, and problems experienced were measured. Not a single table in either monographic report presents a comparison of the widowed with other groups in the samples (National Council on the Aging, 1975, 1981).

This class of studies is not vulnerable to the errors from "labeling" that characterized the three other classes. The common neglect of the variable of widowhood surely shows that it is not in the forefront of the minds of the investigators. Indeed, some seem to have forgotten all about it. Accordingly, they would not be casting respondents in that role or mentioning it to the interviewers. The whimsical, unanticipated consequence is an increase in the quality of the buried data. However, this class of studies does have an ultimate, irreduceable deficiency. The generalizations are always limited to the aged, usually those within a particular area. This leads us finally to the new path we have taken in our study.

Secondary Analysis of Nationwide Sample Surveys: A New Path to Knowledge

In nationwide surveys of the general population, young and old widows and widowers from all areas of the country have been sampled and are easily located for secondary analysis by the question on marital status routinely asked. Corresponding control groups of nonwidowed have also been sampled and are located via the same question. Inferences about the effects of widowhood can thus be made safely and have generalizability. Since information on sex and age is also obtained routinely, the essential controls over these factors and the analysis of differential effects in subgroups of the widowed are easily achieved. Since the widowed are a much smaller fraction of the general population than of the aged population, naturally the yield for analysis from any single survey is relatively small. But this obstacle is easily surmounted by using a string of surveys creating, in effect, a supersize-survey. In the bargain one has samples spanning a ·wider range of time and a greater variety of historical conditions, and one dilutes the errors that might operate in a particular survey. Our nine surveys, in totality, yielded 734 widowed individuals which, as the reader will recall from our review, is a far larger sample than has been used in most of the studies of the widowed.

The seven of these surveys that were pooled for the analysis reported in chapter 2 are cross-sectional in design, involving only a single measurement on each individual at a particular point in time. The other two nationwide surveys used for the separate analysis reported in chapter 3 were selected because they are longitudinal in design, involving three measurements on each individual spaced over a four-year period. Thus changes with the prolongation of widowhood or after its onset can be determined. Conventional studies of widowhood involving repeated measurements over time are very rare; the dimension of change, when included, is reconstructed through retrospective questioning, an expedient measure but one more fallible than the genuine measurement of change which, as will be shown, can be incorporated economically through secondary analysis.

In taking this new path, the major problem is that the domain of the effects of widowhood that can be exploited is limited to whatever variables were covered in the original surveys. In contrast with direct inquiries about widowhood that focus on the emotional and adjustmental problems, national surveys of the general population, naturally, do not ask questions about grief and loneliness following the death of a spouse. These are the hypothesized obvious effects of widowhood and are beyond the scope of the original surveys. But this does not mean the variables we were able to locate in such surveys and examine in our study are irrelevant. They may be important, previously neglected, effects of widowhood. The focus of the earlier studies may have narrowed the vision of the investigators. They may never have asked themselves or their respondents whether widowhood reduced interest in the wider world, weakened political involvement, changed ideologies or philosophies of life. It might have seemed the height of impropriety to ask the widows flagrant questions about beneficial effects. Such varied effects, although less poignant than loneliness, mourning, and melancholia, may be just as important scientifically. Secondary analysts must make the most of their inherited wealth, and in this particular instance we have found previously unexplored veins of relevant data. We have also found, surprisingly, measures of many variables, such as unhappiness, that were the focus of earlier studies of widowhood.

The surveys were converted into studies of widowhood only long after they had been completed, the effects being ascertained indirectly through statistical analyses rather than by direct probing. Thus the widowed were never cast as special characters nor was it ever suggested to them that there was supposed to be any connection between widowhood and any of the variables measured. Nor were the interviewers ever alerted to that special status and role. Indeed, they probably did not know who was widowed until far along in, or near the end of, their questioning. A desirable double-blind design was thus insured.

Considering the advantages, one would expect many investigators to have taken this new path. By now it should have become an old well-trodden path to knowledge of widowhood. Instead, one study in the literature stands, as far as we can tell, in spendid isolation. By secondary analysis of a 1963 survey by Almond and Verba of nationwide samples in five countries, Harvey and Bahr (1974) obtained generalizable cross-national findings on the variable of misanthropy.[11]

The analyses in chapters 2 and 3 are confined to widows. Since differential effects among widows and widowers have been amply documented, merging the two groups in one analysis would create obscurity. Ambiguity would also arise unless sex were controlled since the widowed and control groups of non-widowed differ strikingly in their proportions of men and women. Widows do not necessarily have more severe problems. Any such generalizations remain to be established by adequate nationwide data. However, by their sheer numbers they are the larger social problem and are therefore given priority in our study. A brief treatment of the effects among widowers is reported separately in chapter 4.

In appraising any survey findings on the effects of widowhood—whether based on secondary or primary analysis—the risk of error of an unusual nature must be considered. Those for whom widowhood was so intolerable that they became permanently hospitalized, or were driven to suicide, or died from natural causes set in motion by the bereavement can no longer answer any surveyor's questions. Given such a brutish process involving the attrition of the weakest and the survival of only the fittest, survey findings, some might argue, must show a false and too rosy picture of the effects of widowhood.

That there is the danger of some error cannot be denied by those using any variety of survey method. The three cases presented earlier testify to the trauma of widowhood. The magnitude of the error, however, is the crucial issue and is far less than one might fear. Those very cases that testified to trauma were drawn from three different surveys and gave their testimony in the ordinary course of the inquiries. Thus, early in her text Lopata rightly reports that attrition is low: "Yet, in spite of some tendencies in that direction, most women do not become fatally ill, commit suicide, or become institutionalized in mental hospitals after the death of the husband" (1973: 75). Such qualitative evidence that the error is small is only suggestive. However, the vital statistics Lopata cites also imply that attrition is low, and serve as well to remind us how long the burdens of widowhood must be carried. "Three-fourths of the women who become widows at age 45 can expect to live an additional 25 years . . . . Of the widows bereft of their spouse at age 65, somewhat more than half can expect to live 15 years longer and about a third still have 20 years of life before them" (1973: 21).

Powerful quantitative evidence is provided by a rigorous and comprehensive study of mortality that traced the fates of four thousand white widowed individuals over a twelve-year period. Mortality was not significantly higher for widows than for married women after proper statistical controls on the differences in age and other characteristics were introduced. However, both the crude and adjusted mortality rates were significantly higher for widowers than for married men (Helsing, et al., 1981). Thus the findings presented in chapters 2 and 3 on widows, the major focus of our study, are relatively free from "survivor bias." The contrasted, gloomy findings on widowers, as we shall explain in detail in chapter 4, become more compelling when one realizes that they are based on the relatively healthy survivors who could be studied in the surveys.[12]

Two additional safeguards against the risk are incorporated in our study. For the one set of data on widows potentially most vulnerable to this source of error used in chapter 3, we could determine the attrition due to mortality and institutionalization. That evidence warrants confidence in the set of findings. Including a control group throughout the study provides a final safeguard. Just as there are some who cannot survive widowhood, so, too, there are others who cannot survive marriage. The presence of some spouses—the worst kind—may well create as much trauma for the partner as the death of even the best kind of spouse. Surely, everyday experience and the divorce rate tell the truth of these assertions. Thus, when the effects of widowhood are documented by the differences between widowed and married, two selected, relatively healthy groups of survivors are involved. If the absolute findings among the widowed are too rosy, it matters little. In effect, that error is discounted or subtracted by comparison with the too rosy findings among the married, thus avoiding false conclusions. Studies that lack a control group provide no rigorous way to discount the absolute findings and the error—albeit trivial for widows—stands.

Three brief points should be noted before introducing the findings. All of the analyses are confined to effects of widowhood among whites. This is not to suggest that the effects among blacks are any the less severe and that these do not deserve attention and amelioration. For many technical reasons to be reviewed, that analysis has been postponed, but we hope it will be carried forward by others who will take the new path to knowledge of those effects.

The findings have many theoretical implications and practical applications, but commentary and speculation on such matters have been kept to a minimum. Matters methodological and of an intricate technical character are also omitted from the text but are not slighted and are treated fully in the notes.

One last point. The mode of analysis employed was chosen not only for its appropriateness, but for the clarity and simplicity with which a very large number of findings could be presented. Other modes of statistical analysis were considered but rejected on one or another of these grounds.

2. Nationwide Cross-sectional Surveys

The findings on the effects of widowhood presented in this chapter are based on seven nationwide surveys conducted by the National Opinion Research Center of the University of Chicago (hereafter referred to as NORC). Each spring from 1972 to 1978 NORC completed its annual *General Social Survey*, a continuing inquiry sponsored by the National Science Foundation to serve the varied needs of social scientists and policy makers for reliable information on many characteristics of the general population, and on social trends.[1] Since the aggregate results have been published annually and the data tapes distributed at low cost for scholars to use in teaching and research, the surveys have been exposed to substantial scientific scrutiny.

The General Social Survey employed rigorous forms of area-probability sampling of the noninstitutionalized, English-speaking population of the continental United States, eighteen years of age or older.[2] Thus all kinds of widows— young and old, bereaved recently or long ago, poor and rich, merry and sad, those about to remarry and others committed or resigned to widowhood—would be included in these samples, and in their proper proportions. So long as they were alive and at large, their health and their English not so poor as to prevent an interview, they would have been incorporated in the surveys. Then they were easily located for our special study by the question on marital status routinely asked in the seven surveys.

What is equally important, in light of the earlier review, is that a control group composed of the nationwide sample of married individuals contained within the surveys was also located for study, comparative analysis revealing the patterns that distinguished the widowed.[3] A second comparison or control group, completely neglected in past studies of the widowed despite its value, was readily located to isolate the distinctive effects of widowhood. This group was composed of the nationwide sample of divorced or separated individuals contained within the surveys. They too had lost or relinquished a spouse, although less irrevocably than the widowed and for reasons that are varied and sometimes welcomed but surely different. Whatever the circumstances, they nevertheless are bereft and the distinctive effects of the bereavement of widowhood can be isolated by the comparisons. The pitfalls of the pseudocomparative design reviewed earlier were thus avoided, and a truly comparative design containing two control groups was extracted from the original surveys. Pooling the seven surveys increased the size of the three groups, strengthening the statistical base for the findings. Indeed, the final sizes, even after the groups were refined and "purified" in ways described later were larger than the numbers used in most of the surveys and case studies of widowhood in the literature. And by combining surveys over the years 1972–78, the results no longer were vulnerable to transient conditions that might have influenced the behavior of the widowed or affected the operation of a particular survey.

The effects of widowhood revealed by the comparisons of the three groups had to be measured, naturally, by the questions that happened to be included in the surveys. As the name implies, these were general social surveys, omnibus in content, in order to cater to the diverse needs and interests of social scientists. They also served our special needs very well. Five areas in which it is plausible that widowhood has effects and which have figured prominently in past studies were covered. The emotional aftermath of bereavement, so central in past research, is treated under the heading "feeling tone," and the other areas covered are social involvement, finances, health, and what we titled "outlook on life and society." Taken altogether, effects were explored over a broad domain, and examined by the multiple questions or indicators that, fortunately, were available in most areas. Thus we were not left at the mercy of a single, possibly biased and certainly narrow item, and the reliability and comprehensiveness of measurement were enhanced.

All the questions were chosen blindly, prior to examining the results obtained for the three groups, so as to avoid any insidious tendency to invent a reason for rejecting items that disconfirmed some favorite hypothesis. However, enough questions were available so that we could objectively select those items that would yield sensitive and unbiased measurements and longer batteries that would be balanced in content and format. To ask a widow or any other respondent only whether she is sad and whether life is dreary is to accentuate the negative. It may seem perverse, but one might just as well ask "Are you happy?" or "What benefits have you gained from your husband's death" which accentuate the positive. It would seem best to construct or, in the case of secondary analysis, to select questions that give an equal chance for positive and negative effects to be entered into the score as, for example, a scale for rating the level of happiness or the quality of life. It is not being heartless, mindless, or insensitive to the plight of the widowed to follow this strategy; it is fair, and that is what we have tried to be.

NORC is notable for the high quality of its sampling and measurement procedures. Indeed, it was the very agency Lopata chose to conduct her first survey of Chicago widows. Those high-quality services cost us nothing as secondary analysts. Moreover, the funding and the continuing nature of this series of surveys provided time and resources to test and improve procedures. Special care would be likely in surveys so public, so highly visible, serving so sophisticated a constituency. The surveys have stood up well under scrutiny. NORC's concern and care is also suggested by the expert committee of scholars who have been advisors throughout the years. It is attested by the methodological experiments on the quality of sampling and measurement, the results of which warrant confidence in the original surveys and, in turn, in the particular subsamples and data extracted to examine the effects of widowhood.[4] Accidents, of course, can afflict a survey and errors can undermine its accuracy, but we are heavily insured against such occasional risks by using seven surveys.

Purifying the Groups

The difficulties in drawing sound and subtle conclusions from the comparisons were reduced by reference to the elaborate measurements of personal characteristics also available in the surveys. Features commonly noted—sex, age, race, education, religion, residential location—plus features often neglected in surveys—income, number of children, household size and composition, social origins, etc.—could be described. Such information was used initially to refine and purify the groups used in the design, and later to draw elaborate profiles of the three groups as an aid in interpreting the findings. One should sense the initial crudity and impurity in our three groups, and also in the groups used in past surveys and case studies of widowhood, although often it is not noticed. The question on marital status in all surveys measures the current situation, not the past history. In any comparison involving the currently married, some are in fact remarried and they share with the widowed and divorced groups the experience of having been bereaved either through earlier widowhood or divorce. Although it is now behind them, the effects might have lingered on. Being "married" therefore does not have the simple, unitary meaning it might seem to have to some investigators using such a control group, and they would underestimate the effects of widowhood or divorce. The more such impurities in the control group of married, the greater the underestimation of the effects.

The widowed group also contains impurities. Some of them might have been married, then divorced, then remarried, and now widowed. Their previous divorces, rather than or as well as their widowhood might account for the effects observed. That pattern of experience is rare among the widowed, but perfectly understandable and a possible source of impurity. However, there is another pattern of past experience that may also lead to impurities in the widowed group, which at first may seem confusing. There is an inherent ambiguity in the concepts "widowed" and "divorced or separated," or at least in the way people think about those terms and about themselves. The ambiguity even slips into the Oxford Dictionary, which defines a widow as "a woman whose husband is dead (and who has not married again.)" (Vol. 12: 112). It does not add "and who was not separated or divorced from him." Some women whose former husbands or separated husbands have died describe themselves as "widowed" and others still think of themselves as "divorced or separated." The few investigators who have noted the problem and who have been thoughtful enough to have a method for identifying such anomalous or impure cases sometimes classify them one way, sometimes the other way.

In an essay on grief, based on her well designed sample survey of widows aged fifty or older in metropolitan Chicago, Lopata reported the surprising fact that a "full 46 percent of the older widows felt that they themselves and their social life were unaffected by the husband's death." She then remarks, "Least affected are women who, by choice, were *no longer living with their husbands or ex-husbands at the time of their death.* Women who were separated from their husbands through external circumstances—armed services or occupational assignments—vary in their responses, depending on whether they had built an independent life for themselves, found husband substitutes, or remained 'waiting wives'" (1975: 44, italics supplied).[5] It is only implied, but it is clear that these respondents defined themselves as "widows," and that Lopata, with full awareness, also treated them as widows eligible to remain in her sample. But what is also clear from her findings is that when such cases are buried within the control group of "divorced and separated," there also might be underestimation, since such individuals may show effects from the death of the husband.

The ambiguity of the concepts and the dilemma in deciding on the appropriate classification are conveyed by the contrasting decision Glick, Weiss, and Parkes made in their study of a sample of recently widowed in Boston drawn from death records. They note: "*Not all those* who agreed to participate proved *eligible and suitable.* A number had been separated from the spouse at the time of the spouse's death" (1974: 22, italics supplied).[6]

Fortunately, the elaborate measurement of personal characteristics enabled us to locate many of the impure cases. Our decision was to purify the groups as much as possible so as to measure the maximum effects of widowhood. The impurities that could not be removed by the direct measurement of cases with anomalous histories were then reduced by refining the groups in various ways we shall describe. Some impure cases still remain within the final groups but their number, fortunately, can be determined by other background questions that were asked, and whether they have unduly weighted our findings can be evaluated. These various stages of purification, refinement, and evaluation of the groups in the final design will be reviewed.

NORC had asked everyone the background question whether they had ever been divorced or separated. Any members of the married group whose previous marriages had ended in divorce or whose current marriages involved any experience of separation were eliminated from the final group. Any members of the widowed group who answered "yes" (those whose previous marriage had ended in divorce plus those of the anomalous type who had been married only once and had lost the "spouse" from whom they were divorced or separated) were eliminated. The widowed group thus is thoroughly pure in composition, and the married group has been purified to a considerable extent.

The married group, however, still contained individuals whose previous marriages had ended in widowhood and who had subsequently remarried. And the divorced or separated group still contained two sources of impurity. It included those whose experience involved the sequence: married-widowed-remarried-divorced or separated, and the anomalous type with the sequence: married-divorced or separated-death of ex-spouse or separated spouse. NORC had not asked the background question whether a spouse had ever died in all of the surveys, but fortunately that question was asked beginning with the 1978 survey. Thus those sources of impurity cannot be eliminated throughout by any direct and simple screening procedure. The impure cases remain within the two final groups, but they are not buried. Since all the surveys cover the identical universe and use the same basic sampling design, the number can be estimated from the results of the question in the two surveys. Fortunately they are few and their weight upon our findings is negligible. The refinement of the groups helped to reduce the number, and that process will be reviewed before reporting the magnitude of the impurities in the final groups.[7]

Refining the Groups

As noted in the introduction, all of the analyses in this chapter are confined to women. Thus sex is automatically controlled in the comparisons. The danger of spurious conclusions in a study of unrefined groups, where the married group is half men and the divorced also include a large proportion of men whereas the widowed are predominantly women, thus was avoided. The findings also become sharply focused on effects among widows, not upon the more abstract and vague, albeit general category of all the widowed. (Effects among widowers, however, have not been ignored and will be treated separately, though briefly, in chapter 4.) Insofar as respondents, whether married or widowed, would be more likely to speak candidly, reveal their private pains or secret pleasures to an interviewer of the same sex, the validity of the findings is also increased by confining the analyses to women. Since the interviewers in most surveys are predominantly women, willy-nilly most women respondents will be interviewed by women and most men will be interviewed by someone of the opposite sex.[8]

These were the main reasons for the exclusion of men from the three final groups. However, that refinement worked indirectly to eliminate some of the sources of impurity. Widowers and divorced men are much more likely to remarry than widows or divorced women. The odds "favor" a widower about 4:1. Given their lower remarriage rate, the proportion of impure cases with a history of widowhood in a previous marriage contained within the currently married group will be much less in a study confined to women.[9] The currently divorced or separated group, for the same reasons, will also have fewer impure cases with a history of widowhood from a previous marriage in a study limited to women.

As noted in the introduction, all of the analyses are confined to white women. Thus race as well as sex is automatically controlled in the comparisons, and there is no danger of spurious conclusions from that source of difference among the three groups. Although the exclusion of blacks reduces the generality of the findings on the effects of widowhood, it protects the quality of the data in many ways. The effect of widowhood on blacks is, of course, an important problem deserving separate and special attention. However, given the size of the black population, the three groups needed for the analysis would have been only about one-tenth as big as the white groups and the conclusions would have rested on too flimsy a statistical base. In addition, although one can be confident about the sampling of the general population in such surveys, for various reasons the subsamples of the blacks are subject to special biases which might distort or hamper the conclusions. As noted elsewhere, generalizing about blacks from samples restricted to the English-speaking population might not be warranted given the numbers of those who are Hispanic-speaking. And although the attempt is made to assign black interviewers to black respondents because of the clear evidence that their answers are influenced by the race of the interviewer, this safeguard on the quality of the data cannot be instituted in a considerable number of cases.[10]

These were the main reasons for confining the analysis to whites. However, that refinement of the groups also worked indirectly to eliminate some of the impurities. Since husband-absent households are more common in the black population, widows of the anomalous type Lopata described (those not living with their husbands at the time of death or whose former husbands have died) are likely to be fewer in samples confined to whites.

As a result of these refinements, the impurities that could not be eliminated from the final groups were few. In the 1978 survey that asked the question whether (and when) a spouse had died, 3 percent of the currently married white women had been widowed on a previous marriage. Among those currently divorced or separated, 6 percent reported the death of a spouse. This is not to say that all of that latter group were widows in the conventional sense of having experienced bereavement in the course of a previous marriage. Given the ambiguities reviewed, some might have been referring to the death of the husbands from whom they were currently divorced or separated. (The estimates from the 1980 survey, 4 percent and 8 percent of the respective groups reporting the death of a spouse, agree closely.) The finding of very few former widows in the married group (3–4 percent), though based on only two surveys, is consistent with the large-scale evidence cited and again suggests that "survivor bias" from remarriage creates little risk to our study of widows.

The groups were refined in one other way. As noted in the introduction, in any gross comparisons of the married, widowed, and divorced, implicitly one is comparing the young and the middle-aged with the old. The married on the average are much younger than the widowed, and the divorced fall in between in age. Therefore age was controlled, to avoid spurious conclusions about the effects of widowhood, partly by a further refinement of the three groups of white women, excluding those under age forty and those eighty years of age or older. Fortunately, very few white women are widowed at so young an age, and less than 2 percent of the widows in our original sample were under age forty. Sadly, widowhood becomes progressively more common with age. Indeed it is so common that there were hardly any married women left in our total sample at age eighty, and it would have been impossible to implement a satisfactory comparative design. It seemed the wise precaution to exclude those age eighty or older because of possible biases in the sampling of the very old.[11] Within that range, age forty to seventy-nine, separate comparisons of the three groups were made for those age forty to fifty-nine, and those age sixty to seventy-nine.

In that way, three goals were achieved. Relatively tight control over age was imposed; the married, widowed, and divorced or separated who were compared falling within the same age band. And circumscribed effects that were specific to one group of widows, the younger or older, or that were intensified in the one group and attenuated in the other, could also be demonstrated.[12] Such differential effects have often been reported in the literature. By controlling age in this fashion rather than in other ways, generalizable evidence on the problem based on nationwide samples could be obtained. Thirdly, since very young widows (those under forty) are most likely to remarry and the rate declines progressively to almost zero among those over fifty-nine, the refinement by age automatically reduces the impurities in the married and divorced groups. Then whatever remaining small impurities affect the findings can be located because of the division into two age levels and applied almost exclusively to the younger group. (To put it another way, the "survivor bias" from remarriage is automatically reduced and circumscribed.)

In summary, what lay hidden within these surveys and was extracted for secondary analysis was a comparative study of nationwide samples of white widows, and control groups of married and the divorced or separated white women, all within the same age bands covering a broad domain of possible effects of widowhood.

Profiles of Widows and Married and Divorced or Separated Women

Prior to examining effects, profiles of the three groups were drawn based on the elaborate measurement of personal characteristics in the surveys. Inspection of the profiles enabled us to take additional precautions, if needed, to control other sources of spurious conclusions, and it enlarged our knowledge of the constellation of features distinguishing the widows that might account for the effects.

Separate profiles were drawn for the younger and older members of each group as an aid to understanding any age differential effects. One should recognize that such effects may have complex origins and that some obscurity is bound to surround their interpretation even after elaborate analysis. Primary and secondary analysts share the predicament of not being able to untangle completely the complex web of factors that may be involved: the financial obligations and circumstances, the family obligations and domestic arrangements, the recency of bereavement. Some of these factors will be examined and their contribution isolated by special analyses. Ultimately, one must acknowledge that age itself is complex and obscure in meaning, that younger and older widows differ not only in the stage of the life-cycle they have reached but also in the generations they represent. They grew up and married in different historical periods, and they may have been widowed during periods when society's treatment of widows was different. Therefore they may not perceive the bereavement they have in common in the same way. The two components of the complex, age, cannot be untangled by the analyses in this chapter, and we shall reserve any subtle conclusions as to the nature of such effects until chapter 3, which does open an avenue to examine generational factors.

Before presenting the profiles one important feature, measured only in 1978 in the one survey containing the two questions on whether and when the respondent had ever been widowed or divorced or separated, is essential background. Among the young widows, 15 percent had been bereaved for less than one year, 46 percent for more than five years. Among old widows, 10 percent had been bereaved for less than one year, and 65 percent for more than five years. (Since these estimates were based on the very small numbers in the one survey from 1978, the 1980 survey, which fortunately contained the same question, was used as a check. The agreement between the estimates was very high. For example, among the old widows in the 1980 survey 63 percent had been widowed for more than five years.) Among the young divorced or separated 7 percent had lost their husbands in that fashion within the last year, and 50 percent had sustained that loss more than five years ago. Among the old, 4 percent had experienced that loss within the last year and 74 percent earlier than five years ago.

Table 2.1 shows the profiles of older and younger married, widowed, and divorced or separated white women, arranging their features for clarity under three headings: personal characteristics, current milieu, and childhood milieu. The items included under each heading were chosen because empirical evidence and theory suggest either that they might modify or mediate the effects of widowhood, or that they could separately, independently, influence the outcomes we shall examine later and, depending on their distributions among married and widowed, therefore have to be considered or controlled to avoid spurious conclusions. (Since the data are pooled over the series of surveys, conditions peculiar to a given year or annual survey are balanced out.)

Before inspecting the profiles from these perspectives, consider another useful purpose served by the data in table 2.1. Since there is independent authoritative information on the distribution of such characteristics in the general population in its older and younger strata, the age differences in the table provide a test of the quality of the surveys and the validity of our data. Thus for example, because of the expansion of educational opportunity in America in modern times, age cohorts born more recently are known to have higher educational attainment, and this fact is reproduced in our data. In each marital status

Table 2.1. The profiles of widowed, married, and divorced or separated white women (pooled data, NORC annual surveys, 1972–78)

N^a =	Age 60–79			Age 40–59		
	Married 439	Widowed 346	Divorced or separated 76	Married 1065	Widowed 118	Divorced or separated 159
Personal characteristics						
Total family income last year^b						
Median	$7,590	$3,940	$4,580	$15,800	$7,690	$7,950
25th percentile	4,860	2,640	3,110	10,900	4,667	4,375
Educational attainment						
8th grade or less	35%	43%	28%	13%	19%	18%
grades 9—12	47	38	53	63	60	52
More than twelve	18	19	19	24	21	30
Current religious affiliation						
Protestant	70%	71%	82%	64%	58%	70%
Catholic	23	24	12	30	32	25
Jewish	4	3	5	3	5	—
None	3	1	1	2	3	3
Number of children (living or dead)						
None	15%	16%	15%	6%	14%	12%
One	16	15	24	10	14	9
Two	28	27	21	27	17	21
Three or more	42	43	41	57	55	58
Current milieu						
Household size						
One person	1%	75%	63%	^{c}	38%	36%
Two	83	15	26	32	26	25
Three or more	16	10	11	67	36	40
Composition						
Zero members under six	100%	99%	99%	95%	97%	95%
Zero members six to twelve	99	97	93	75	85	77
Zero members thirteen to seventeen	98	95	97	57	68	63

Table 2.1. (continued)

	Age 60–79			Age 40–59		
N^a =	Married 439	Widowed 346	Divorced or separated 76	Married 1065	Widowed 118	Divorced or separated 159
Region living in currently						
South	33%	35%	32%	31%	26%	27%
West	8	8	22	10	13	22
North	59	57	46	59	61	51
Size of place living in currently						
Large city	14%	18%	28%	12%	16%	25%
Open country	23	14	13	19	11	9
Childhood milieu						
Father's occupation during childhood						
Median prestige score[e]	43	43	44	42	43	42
Farmer or farm laborer	39%	39%	38%	24%	18%	22%
Father's education[d]						
Eighth grade or less	77%	71%	70%	61%	66%	54%
Grades 9–12	15	20	17	28	22	26
More than 12	8	9	13	11	12	20
Mother's education[d]						
Eighth grade or less	73%	68%	72%	54%	63%	45%
Grades 9–12	20	26	20	36	24	40
More than 12	7	6	8	10	13	15
Number of siblings (living or dead)[f]						
None	5%	6%	5%	6%	5%	11%
One	8	10	11	16	5	16
Two—five	43	41	46	49	57	50
Six or more	44	45	38	30	33	23

Family composition at age 16						
Not living with own father and mother	16%	24%	24%	17%	18%	27%
Reason						
Death of parent	87%	85%	67%	67%	67%	51%
Divorce or separation	9	9	28	24	29	42
Other	4	6	5	9	4	7
	100%	100%	100%	100%	100%	100%
Region living in at age 16						
South	31%	34%	33%	30%	27%	30%
West	3	4	13	5	9	9
North	63	57	50	60	60	56
Foreign country	4	5	4	5	4	6
Native birth [g]	93%	94%	95%	93%	100%	92%
Religion raised in [h]						
Protestant	71%	72%	73%	71%	61%	66%
Catholic	23	23	15	23	34	34
Jewish	4	4	4	3	1	—
None	2	2	7	3	3	—

a. Depending on the characteristic, the bases used for the computation of percentages vary slightly from the Ns shown because respondents occasionally gave no answer to one or another question. Whenever the numbers that had to be excluded were of more than trivial magnitude, it will be noted.

b. About 3 percent of the younger and 6 percent of the older respondents refused to report income, and the bases are correspondingly reduced.

c. Less than one percent.

d. In about one-fifth of the younger and one-third of the older respondents, the parent's education could not be ascertained for various reasons (fading of memory after so many years, etc.). The bases for the percentages shown are correspondingly reduced.

e. The Hodge-Siegel-Rossi scale was used to score the prestige of the specific occupations reported.

f. The question was worded in a fashion that included step-sibs and adoptive sibs in the count.

g. The question was asked in only two of the annual surveys, and the bases correspondingly are reduced by about 75 percent.

h. The question was not included in the 1972 survey. The bases correspondingly are reduced by about 14 percent.

group, the younger cohort is far more likely to have gone beyond elementary school. For the same historical reason, the parents of earlier cohorts have lower educational attainment than parents of more recent age cohorts, and our data conform to this established fact. Similarly, because of the growth of urbanization, older cohorts are more likely to have grown up in farm families, which is also borne out in our data for each marital status group. A sad fact in America is that the old are poor, and this is vividly demonstrated in our table. In each marital status group, family income is much lower among the old. For example, median annual income for the year prior to the survey was $7,690 for younger widows but only $3,940 for older white widows, a poor basis for managing in the years 1971–77. One standard for judgment is the "poverty line." In 1974 (the midpoint of the time span) it was set at $2,352 for a single person. Thus, as shown, about a quarter of the old widows would have officially been defined as living in poverty. Admittedly, assets as well as income have to be considered for a full appraisal. That evidence, presented in a lengthy note rather than in the table, does not change the verdict.[13]

With confidence in the data fortified by these and more stringent checks,[14] now compare the profiles of the married, widowed, and divorced or separated women for their bearing on the later analysis of the effects of widowhood. In many ways, especially among older women, the profiles of the widowed and married are very similar. The distributions of current religious affiliation and the region in which they now live, their regional and rural origins, native birthplace, the prestige of father's occupation and educational level of father, the religion in which they were raised—all show negligible or, at most, modest differences as would be expected.[15] Live long enough, and death comes to every quarter and makes widows of them all.

There is, however, one constellation of features, especially among the young, where the profiles of the married and widowed differ. The average income of the married is almost double that of the widowed among older women, and more than double among the younger women. And the married women had a modest advantage in education as did their mothers (in the case of the young), came from smaller families, and were less likely to be reared as Catholics. The image cast by these data, and confirmed by the literature, is a vicious, accelerating downward spiral. It is well established that the poor die younger. Our younger widows came from less advantaged families and thus made less advantageous marriages. Then they were at greater risk of becoming widowed at an early age and left with meager resources. But the handicap they started with is too small to account for the very large differences documented in "current" (1970s) income. A bit poorer to start with, they must have become very much poorer as a consequence of their widowhood.[16]

The subtle social-psychological effects we shall examine later may simply reflect the harsh economic conditions which widows suffer, their changed circumstances acting as the main intervening variable or crucial link in a chain of effects. We shall test this model of the process. However, since the economic plight to some small degree precedes rather than follows widowhood there is also the danger—albeit small—of spurious conclusions, the outcomes we observe being caused by prior poverty rather than widowhood. In any case, the mode of analysis employed will serve both to prevent spurious conclusions and to trace a complex process.

There is a second constellation of features that differentiates widows from the married. Among the old, most of whose children would have long since grown up and left the household, the widowed are far more likely to live alone. Three-quarters of them have such a milieu in contrast with 1 percent of the married. The married live predominantly in two-person households, as would be expected given their age and the probable age of their children. As the data on household composition reveal, the minority of old married in three-person or larger households and the minority of old widows in two-person or larger households almost never live with young children. Given their advanced age, even their grandchildren would be likely to be older than seventeen.

Among women age forty to fifty-nine, the same patterns are foreshadowed and the contrast, though not as dramatic, is sharp. About a third of the widows live alone in contrast with less than half of one percent among the married.[17] The younger married are far more likely than the older married to live in three-person or larger households, but the children present (as one would expect) are predominantly thirteen or older. Among the widows who do not live alone, the majority live in three-person or larger households, but children, when present, are mainly thirteen or older.[18]

Living alone, obviously an effect of widowhood that is widespread, may be another link in a chain that leads to more subtle social and psychological effects. To be sure, it does not necessarily mean continual social isolation, since there may be frequent visits between households, between grown children and their widowed mothers, between widows and neighbors or friends. In this connection, the datum on number of children (although, in the phrasing of the one question that was asked, including children ever born, whether now living or dead) is relevant. Almost all of the women have (or had) at least one child, and close to three-quarters of them have (or had) two or more children. Children, of course, create companionship but also an economic burden which, given their poverty, would be hard for widows to bear. But certainly the data on household composition suggest that these, for the most part, are not the burdens (or benefits) created by very young, dependent children. Granted the complexity of the consequences of their having children, the later analysis enables us to examine the ways it mediates and modifies other effects.[19]

In passing, it might be noted that although widows and married were equally likely to have started their lives on the farm, their later destinations are different. Widows are somewhat less likely to be living in "open country," presumably that milieu being difficult or uncongenial for them.

Since our design for evaluating the distinctive effects produced by widowhood involves comparisons with those who have lost a husband through divorce or separation, the prominent features of the profile of that group should also be noted as a prelude to the analysis of effects. Perhaps the most important feature to note is that divorced women share equally the economic situation of the widowed, the differences in median income being negligible and both groups being much poorer than their married counterparts. The stereotype of the rich widow or the rich divorcee is just that: a false picture of their circumstances. An ironic feature of the situation is that the divorced are the most educated of the three groups, which should give them some advantage in the labor market, and, among the young, come from families with more education. Despite these early advantages, they have become poor.[20] The divorced also share equally with widows the situation of living alone.

Although it is not our main theme, a substantive finding of note is that the divorced are far more likely than the other two groups to have grown up in homes broken by divorce or separation. (The same finding was demonstrated by Pope and Mueller (1976: 56, table 2) for white women using national survey data.) And although all three groups started their lives in the same locations, the later destination of the divorced is more likely to be the West coast and the big city.

General Effects of Widowhood

Table 2.2 examines potential effects of widowhood in the five areas covered.

Feeling Tone

The first area, titled "feeling tone" parallels the main, frequently exclusive focus of many past studies that treat the immediate, painful emotional aftermath of bereavement. Indeed the widowed are significantly less likely than the married to describe their lives as "very happy" and "exciting".[21] The finding may appear too obvious, but note in contrast with the picture of gloom painted in past studies that only a small minority say that life is truly "dull" or select the bottom category "not too happy" on the rating scale. And in these respects they are no worse off than the divorced women.[22] Surely that is surprising since, in some instances, the divorced deliberately acted to free themselves from unhappy marriages and in most instances had some element of choice before the divorce could be arranged. Although the situation is not of their making, some of the widows also may be freed from bad marriages and their happiness and lives then enhanced. The memorable cases reported in a study of the older widowed come to mind:

One man said: "When my wife died I felt a little lonely for a short time, but this was nothing compared to the relief I felt. I feel a lot better now because I don't have the burden of a trouble-making gold-digger on my head. Before she died, my stomach was always upset and I was always constipated. Now I have never enjoyed better health. I'm free and I'm going to stay this way."

A woman said, "I never had any feelings for my husband and I paid dearly with emotional tensions and unhappiness all through the years of my married life. Now at last I'm free to live my life my way—what's left of it" (Cosneck, 1970: 371–72).[23]

Feelings surrounding specific spheres of life are shown in the next three items in the table. As expected, widows are significantly less likely to report a "great deal" or "very great deal" of satisfaction with their family life than their married counterparts. But, once again, only a small minority of widows report extreme dissatisfaction and they are no more dissatisfied than the divorced. That negative feelings do not float over or suffuse all realms of life is suggested by the next items. Satisfaction with the place in which they live is less frequent among younger widowed and divorced than among the married, but none of the differences, among old or young, is significant. And the only significant difference between marital status groups in the satisfaction derived from friendships is the slightly lower level among the young divorced.

That the emotional problems of women who have lost a husband either through widowhood or divorce are more severe among the young is also documented. Consistently, the disparity between the married and these two bereft groups is greater in magnitude among the young than the old, and careful inspection of the data will show that this is not because there is a decline in satisfaction as people age. The married, despite advanced age, have not converged upon the widowed and are no less happy than "young marrieds". Rather it is that the young who lack a husband, whatever the reason, have diverged from their married counterparts, but again it should be stressed that negative feelings are not the modal or prevalent pattern even among the younger widows and divorcees.

These findings are surprisingly mild in tone—not that they give great comfort—in contrast with the harsh tone in much of the literature. The narrow universes covered, the small samples and biased sampling procedures, the pseudo-comparative research designs and lack of control groups or inadequate controls, the structuring of the interview so as to heighten the saliency of the role of widow to respondent and interviewer—these and other methodological features of past studies may account for the discrepant findings. One should also stress that many of the earlier studies cornered their subjects within weeks or months of their widowhood, whereas our subjects, as earlier noted, are long past that point. Freud's distinction fits. Those studies explored mourning, short-term effects. Ours explores melancholia. Protracted depressing effects evidently are rare.

Outlook on Life

It is a reasonable hypothesis that those whom fate has dealt a heavy, irremediable blow would have developed a lasting sour outlook on life and society. The

Table 2.2. The effects of widowhood revealed by comparisons of widowed, married, and divorced or separated white women (Pooled data, NORC annual national surveys, 1972–78)

	Age 60-79			Age 40-59		
N =	Married 439	Widowed 346	Divorced or separated 76	Married 1065	Widowed 118	Divorced or separated 159
I. Feeling Tone						
Overall happiness (self-rating)						
Very happy	49%	27%***	28%***	44%***	14%***	19%***
Pretty happy	43	57	55	48	60	59
Not too happy	8	17	17	7	26	22
Find life generally[a]						
Exciting	37%	31%***	37%*	42%*	29%*	27%***
Pretty Routine	60	57	51	55	64	63
Dull	3	12	12	3	7	10
Satisfaction with family life[b]						
Great deal or very great deal	84%	68%***	55%***	86%***	67%***	60%***
Some-quite a bit	15	26	32	13	27	34
Little or none	1	6	14	1	6	6
Satisfaction with place living in[b]						
Great deal or very great deal	69%	68%	63%	60%	47%	52%
Some-quite a bit	29	30	32	36	45	40
Little or none	2	2	5	4	8	7
Satisfaction with friendship[b]						
Great deal or very great deal	78%	77%	71%	78%	72%	67%**
Some-quite a bit	21	22	25	21	23	31
Little or none	1	1	4	1	5	2
II. Outlook						
Misanthropy scale[c]						
Most people can be trusted	43%	40%	25%***	54%	45%	41%*
People try to be helpful	58	61	42[e]	63	59	56
Most people take advantage	22	26	37[e]	22	36**	34**

Anomia scale						
Hardly fair to bring child into world[a]	41%	43%	42%	36%	37%	50%*
Can't help wondering whether anything is worthwhile[d]	41	47	38	38	50	55*
Have to live for today and let tomorrow take care of itself[d]	51	50	62	42	48	59*
The lot of the average man is getting worse[a]	54	54	52	58	54	67
No right and wrong ways to make money[d]	30	26	28	20	26	24
III. Social involvement						
Spend social evening with relatives[a]						
once a week or more often	33%	45%**	33%	39%	45%	36%
Several times a year or less often	35	21	33	26	29	25
Spend social evening with neighbors[a]						
Once a week or more often	23%	35%e	33%	23%	27%**	37%***
Several times a year or less often	51	42	41	49	33	45
Spend social evening with friends[a]						
Once a week or more often	12%	13%	19%	13%	20%*	23%***
Several times a year or less often	54	55	52	44	52	38
Go to a bar or tavern[a]						
Once a week or more often	2%	3%	7%*	4%	8%	13%***
Several times a year or less often	96	96	91	88	83	66
Number of voluntary association memberships[a]						
Zero	33%	30%	41%	22%	38%*	33%*
One	35	36	26	26	24	23
Two or more	32	35	33	52	38	44
Attend religious services						
Never	8%	10%	20%**	8%	17%*	16%***
Several times a year or less	27	24	38	25	27	36
Once or twice a month	14	15	9	15	10	13
Nearly every week or every week	42	40	24	41	33	29
More than once a week	11	11	9	11	13	6

Table 2.2. (continued)

	Age 60–79			Age 40–59		
N =	Married 439	Widowed 346	Divorced or separated 76	Married 1065	Widowed 118	Divorced or separated 159
Hours of television viewing per day[a]						
Zero	2%	5%	—	4%	2%	9%
Four or more	40	38	36	26	31	20
Median	2.8	2.7	2.6	2.5	2.6	2.3
Read the newspaper[a]						
Daily	83%	74%[e]	68%**	78%	74%	63%**
Never	4	4	6	2	5	4
IV. Financial situation						
Getting better last few years	24%	16%**	26%	42%	22%***	29%**
Getting worse	20	25	28	20	35	30
Not at all satisfied with present situation	11%	15%	21%***	15%	24%**	42%***
V. Health						
General health (self-rating)[f]						
Excellent or good	53%	50%	48%	76%	67%	64%***
Fair to poor	47	50	52	24	34	36
Hospitalization or disability in last five years[g]						
None	61%	65%	35%	51%	31%	28%
In two or more years	16	13	17	16	31	35
Satisfaction with health[b]						
Great deal or very great deal	50%	43%	40%	62%	55%	49%***
Some-quite a bit	40	47	47	34	35	37
Little or none	11	10	13	4	10	14

*** Difference between married and widowed (or married and divorced) by two-tailed chi-square test significant at p ≤ 0.001.
** Significant at p ≤ 0.01 > 0.001.
* Significant at p ≤ 0.05 > 0.01.
a. Asked in only four of the seven annual surveys. The bases correspondingly are reduced.
b. Asked in six of the seven annual surveys. A seven-point rating scale was shown the respondent with the three middle points labeled "some," "fair amount," "quite a bit."
c. Asked in five of the seven annual surveys.
d. Asked in only three of the seven annual surveys.
e. By a one-tailed test the difference between married and widowed (or married and divorced) would be significant at the 0.05 level.
f. Asked in six of the seven annual surveys.
g. Asked in only one of the seven annual surveys.

first three items used to test this general hypothesis, shown in section II of the table, constitute one form of Rosenberg's well known "misanthropy" scale which has been found to be a sensitive instrument that discriminates between national populations of different cultures and between groups with different life chances and subcultures. Among the old, the differences between widows and married consistently are negligible and nonsignificant, but in all three tests the divorced are more misanthropic. Among the young, no significant differences are found on two of the three items.[24] On the third item, misanthropy is significantly more prevalent among the widowed than the married, but this hardly constitutes much evidence in favor of the hypothesis. Again we find some indication that the young divorced are more misanthropic, but the evidence is not consistent over all three tests.

In the misanthropy scale, as the term conveys, the negative feelings and ideas are directed at others. Perhaps that accounts for the pattern of our findings. Someone else may have dealt the divorced a dirty blow, but it is fate that has dealt the widows the cruel blow, and on purely rational grounds they have no reason to become misanthropic. Then surely the next five items examined in the table, all drawn from various versions of the well-known "anomia" scale, should capture the very special outlook of widows. Without assigning responsibility, these items assert that life is mean and meaningless, beyond control, and lacks regularity. One would expect widows to agree that "it's hardly fair to bring a child into the world with the way things look for the future."[25] Yet the differences between widowed and married, young or old, are negligible on this and most other items.[26] (Anomia is more prevalent among young divorced, but the differences are not significant among old divorced and show no consistent pattern.) These findings clearly establish that the negative feelings of the widowed have not pervaded their philosophy of life.

Social Involvement

Section III of the table examines the effects of widowhood on various forms of social involvement. On first thought, it would seem plausible that the trauma and depression of widowhood and the loss of a partner who was responsible for some of the widow's former social ties would lead to a decline in involvement. The literature has emphasized this view and documented such effects. Is it not equally plausible, as Lopata has suggested, that widows out of need for new companionship and to mitigate loneliness would try to maintain old ties and develop new ones? Moreover, in light of the inadequate samples in earlier studies and their focus on the immediate aftermath, it would seem wise to re-examine the problem with broader and more extended evidence.

The first four items deal with informal social relations. On several aspects there are significant differences between the married and the widowed. But what should be emphasized is that widows interact more frequently. On other dimensions of informal relations, the differences are negligible and nonsignificant.[27] The divorced, especially the younger ones, have heightened social relations of varied nature outside of the family in contrast with the married.

Social involvement of a formal nature via membership in voluntary associations is examined next in the table. To insure comprehensiveness of measurement NORC asked a battery of questions about memberships in each of fifteen specific kinds of associations, followed by an open-ended probe about "any other kinds of groups or organizations you belong to." Among the old, there are no differences between married and widowed in such social involvement. However, young widows are substantially less likely to have any memberships, and those that do rarely have multiple memberships in contrast with their married counterparts.[28] Thus, although informal social involvement (of some kinds) appears to be heightened by early widowhood, involvement of a formal type is reduced.

Social involvement in the form of attendance at religious services is examined next, using levels of measurement that are refined enough to take account of the subtle and manifold meanings of such conduct and to reveal a possibly complex pattern that might follow widowhood. The variable might signify spiritual as well as (or rather than) social involvement. Then, either the widows might greatly desire the solace they could obtain from going to services or they might reject religion completely—God, in their thoughts, having dealt them a cruel and unjust blow. Thus we might expect widows to show a distinctive bi-modal distribution: those who have rejected religion never going to services and those whose situation is almost inconsolable going several times a week or as often as every day, leaving relatively few Sunday churchgoers in between. That mid-level of observance, conventional in America and conforming to the common pattern, is in good measure social rather than spiritual in character.[29]

Whatever the complexity and obscurity of the variable, there are no differences in the distributions for the older married and widowed. The young widows are less likely to seek the social and spiritual involvement that frequent attendance would give. They have moved, in some degree, in the opposite direction— toward "never" attending. The pattern among the divorced is more sharply contrasted. Their social involvement is least likely to take the form of regular routine attendance at religious services. As might be expected, they are the most likely to go rarely or "never" perhaps reflecting the facts that they were less bound originally by religious sanctions against divorce, and by now have violated the norms and no longer are or feel accepted or welcomed in their church. Taken together, the three variables examined so far consistently show no reduction of social involvement among older widows, but, among the young, involvement of a formal type is reduced by widowhood.

The last two items in section III of the table again have subtle and manifold meanings but clearly are different in character from the first three. Reading a newspaper or watching television can occur in complete isolation and does not produce any direct contact or interaction with other live human beings. But surely such activity connects the individual to the larger social world; brings the person into contact, albeit at a distance, with great events and small happenings involving others.

Some readers, of course, are inclined to see such activity as an anemic form, as an indicator of para-social or pseudosocial rather than true social involvement, as a substitute for or escape from real social life. However, in light of the findings on other forms of social involvement, it would be hard to argue that many widows have escaped from the real social world and have taken refuge in a make-believe world that television might provide. Furthermore, such interpretations of the findings become dubious in light of the way the variable of television is examined. In addition to showing the median number of hours watched, we have chosen two special cutting points along the dimension. One might argue with some plausibility that "four or more hours a day," a figure above the average for mature and old adults, is too much of a good thing, that it displaces other social activities and verges on addiction and escape from real life. In these days of universal ownership of television in America, one might also argue with some plausibility that zero hours of viewing by people other than rarefied critics and aesthetes or the visually handicapped represents avoidance of the larger social world. Whether we examine the average level of TV viewing, or extreme levels suggestive of addiction and escape, it is indubitable that neither widowhood nor divorce in the old or young has any effect on this form of involvement.[30]

Given the mix of information (much of which is ominous in tone) and entertainment in the papers, it is hard to argue that daily reading of that medium provides solace and escape, and it seems reasonable to suggest that never reading the paper indicates lack of involvement with the larger social world. The proportions that fell into these two extreme and revealing categories on the scale used to measure readership are shown next in section III of the table, those in the middle levels ranging from "less than once a week" up to a "a few times a week" being omitted but easily inferred. Young widows are no different from the married in their reading. Old widows show somewhat less social involvement than their married counterparts by this indicator. Although less likely to read the paper every day, as many as three-quarters of them are daily readers and only a tiny fraction—4 percent—among them (no larger than among the married) have eliminated the paper completely from their lives.[31] And the modest effect of widowhood is milder than the effect of divorce; at both age stages, the divorced are considerably less likely to be daily readers of the newspaper.

The ways widowhood might have affected social involvement have been explored by multiple tests covering varied aspects of this sphere. The few effects that were observed were not consistent or large in magnitude and did not impinge uniformly on younger and older widows. And the occasional negative effects of widowhood paled in comparison with those produced by divorce or separation.

Finances

In section IV of table 2.2 the psychological effect of the financial plight of widows is examined. Recall the objective facts presented earlier in table 1: widows' annual income in the previous year was far lower than the income of the married; the disparity was greater among the younger women; and the deprivation relative to the married was as severe among the divorced as among the widowed. The first item in table 2.2, a rating of change in finances in recent years, taps another aspect of their objective situations, and the findings are compatible with those on absolute levels of income. Widows are significantly less likely than the married to report that their situation is improving, and the disparity in the ratings is wider among young widows.

In this context the next finding on their satisfaction with the situation, the psychological response to their circumstances, is dramatic. Among the old, there is no difference between widowed and married in the prevalence of dissatisfaction, and the percentage who answer "not at all satisfied" (the extreme category on the scale presented to them) is unexpectedly small when one realizes how bad their incomes were and how many have experienced a worsening of that bad situation. Age seems to have blunted the actual blow for them and created resignation in response. In contrast, the old divorced show more dissatisfaction. Among younger widows dissatisfaction is significantly greater than among their married counterparts, but once again the extent of dissatisfaction is curiously low in magnitude considering the severity of the situation and the large number of young widows who describe their situation as worsening. Contrasted with the widows, the response of the young divorcee is most emphatic. They are far more likely to express thorough dissatisfaction with their financial situation, even though it is no worse objectively than that of the widowed.

The pattern of the findings on satisfaction with finances closely matches the findings on dissatisfaction with other spheres of life reviewed earlier in section I of the table. The consistency of the findings strengthens the general conclusion. Negative effects of widowhood are modest in magnitude and mild in tone. However valid these findings are psychologically, it should be stressed that they do not validate the moral position that since the plight is not deeply felt, nothing should be done to alleviate it.

Health

The findings relating to health, presented in section V of the table, must be treated cautiously given the risk of "survivor bias" resulting from morbidity and the exclusion from the surveys of those in institutions. Appropriate cautionary notes are attached. Observe first that in each marital status group the old are substantially less likely to rate their general health as "good" or "excellent," which would be expected if the rating was a reflection of the objective fact, the decline in health with advanced age. Such a rating, however, is not purely a report of an objective fact and should not be construed solely in that way. It implicates the person's own standards, the reference group chosen as point of comparison, and the kind of scale one employs to weigh facts and render a judgment. A particular affliction regarded as a minor irritant by one woman can become a major disorder that drives another to invalidism. Thus the rating should be sensitive enough to reveal effects of widowhood that incorporate both objective and subjective aspects of health.

Among the old, widows rate themselves in good or excellent health just as frequently as do the married. However, younger widows are more likely than the married to rate their health as only "fair" or "poor" although the difference is not significant.[32] The finding for the young divorcee is no more negative than that of the widow, but the difference between them and the married is statistically significant.

These findings may seem to contradict the repeated evidence in the literature of increased morbidity following widowhood.[33] What must be stressed again is that the rating of general health is in considerable degree a subjective datum and not an objective report on morbidity.[34] To clarify the issue, we included the next finding in the table, although, unfortunately, it is from only one of the annual national surveys. (Given the smaller numbers in each group, the estimates have a considerable variance.) The two questions used focussed purely on the objective facts by asking: "Have you, yourself, been a patient in a hospital, sanitarium, convalescent or nursing home (apart from having a baby)?" and "Were you unable to work at your job or carry on your regular activities for one month or more because of illness or injury?" The respondent was asked about such hospitalization or disability both in the previous year, and in the four years prior to that. Among the young indeed we now find dramatic confirmation of the literature. They are much more likely than the married to have experienced hospitalization or disability—not only within the last year, but also within the previous four years. Once again, the picture among the younger divorcees is just as gloomy—their morbidity equals that of the widowed.[35]

Despite the objective fact of the high rate of hospitalization and disability among the young widows, and the added fact that their financial problems might make their illnesses truly insupportable, they express almost as much satisfaction with their health as do the married (the difference is not significant), and hardly any of them express extreme dissatisfaction. That only 10 percent of young widows report "little" or "no" satisfaction with their "health and physical condition", when about a third of them have been hospitalized at least twice in the previous five years seems truly surprising. But this latest finding is congruent with the mild dissatisfaction they reported about many other spheres of life.[36] Once again, the young divorced are less satisfied.

The effects explored over a broad domain are generalizable, by virtue of the sampling, to white widows in the 1970s, of all ages from forty to seventy-nine all across the nation and at all stages of distance in time from their earlier bereavement. Indeed, the findings are based on more than one national sample of the noninstitutionalized population, and in most instances on as many as seven well-designed samples.[37] These replicated surveys protect the findings not only from errors of sampling but also from errors of measurement that might occur accidentally in any single inquiry no matter how carefully planned and conducted. And various methodological tests are empirical evidence that measurements of high quality were actually obtained.[38]

The quasi-experimental design imposed after the fact on the surveys—the use of control groups of married and divorced white women of the same ages as the widows—brings us close to isolating effects distinctive to widowhood, but not yet as close as one would like. Although the effects observed were modest in magnitude and mild in tone, nevertheless they might reflect, as noted initially, the financial difficulties and other conditions peculiar to widows but prior to their widowhood. Consequently, the danger of false and exaggerated conclusions about the effects of widowhood still remains. The design employed until now also may have obscured special kinds of effects and produced misleading, although not false, conclusions. If the effects of widowhood were aggravated under such conditions as privation, and attenuated or even obliterated under favorable economic or other conditions, such circumscribed subtle patterns would be submerged or covered over in any overall picture of the general effects of widowhood. By introducing additional controls in the design, these remaining issues as well as processes mediating the effects of widowhood can be examined.[39]

Effects as Related to Privation and Isolation

Table 2.3 examines the effects of widowhood on selected variables at three contrasted levels of income, a low level where both the married and the widowed might well be described as "poor", a high level where, certainly by comparison with the earlier figures of table 2.1, the widowed might be described as "well off", and a middle level. As the reader can see from the size of the cells, widows who are well off are relatively few and, as will be recalled from the distributions in table 2.1, many in the "poor" category are below the poverty line. The first two variables, measures of general feeling-tone, are ones where substantial negative effects of widowhood have been documented by our previous analysis. On the third variable, as expected, the earlier analysis revealed substantially less satisfaction with family life among widows. On the remaining two variables we had previously found surprisingly little difference in satisfaction with finances and health, despite the objective facts that widows indeed suffered greater hardship and, among the young, poorer health whose impact one would expect

Table 2.3. The effects of widowhood as related to income (white women aged 40–79 in the 1972–78 surveys)

$N^a =$	Total annual income under $7,000		Total annual income $7,000–$9,999		Total annual income over $10,000	
	Married 221	Widowed 230	Married 137	Widowed 54	Married 803	Widowed 70
Rating on happiness						
Very happy	45%	23%***	50%	28%*	48%	20%***
Not too happy	9	20	11	17	5	20
Life generally[b]						
Exciting	29	26	35	33	46	39**
Dull	6	13	4	5	2	9
Satisfaction with family life[c]						
Great deal or very great	80	68**	85	76	88	72***
Little or none	1	7	3	4	0	7
Satisfaction with finances						
Not at all satisfied	22	18	20	13	11	19*
Satisfaction with health[c]						
Great deal or very great	47	42	54	59	64	51
Little or none	10	10	7	4	4	7

*** Difference by two-tailed chi-square test significant at $p \leq 0.001$.
** Difference significant at $p \leq 0.01 > 0.001$.
* Difference significant at $p \leq 0.05 > 0.01$.
a. The groups for this analysis are smaller than in earlier tables because information on income, as noted earlier, was not available on some individuals.
b. On this item, the Ns are further reduced by about one-third.
c. On these items, the Ns are reduced by about 15 percent.

to be compounded by poverty. By introducing controls for income, we should be able to see whether the earlier effects on the first three variables are purely mediated by and simply reflect income, or whether those effects are intensified among widows at a particular level of living. For the last two variables, we should be able to reveal circumscribed effects, intensified or operating exclusively at one level, that were obscured in the previous aggregate analysis.[40]

The married, even when poor, are happier than poor widows. And widows, even when well off, have less happy and exciting lives than their married counterparts. Clearly, the sadness widows feel is not simply a reflection of brutish circumstances; oddly enough, privation does not intensify the difference between the two groups. (This is not to deny what the table also shows. Excitement in life, seemingly, has to be bought with money: its frequency increases in both groups as income rises.) The lesser satisfaction with family life among widows is not the product of their financial circumstances. At the same level of income—poor or not—widows are less satisfied than their married counterparts. Yet, when one focuses on the widows at the lowest level of income, who must cope under conditions of privation, extreme dissatisfaction is still the rarity.

This is surely vivid evidence of the temperate way widows react to trouble, and also a testimonial to their strength.

When one examines dissatisfaction with finances at the lower levels of income, there is no evidence of any intensification of effects among widows, the earlier trivial differences persisting even under extreme conditions. If anything, the married at the two lower levels of income show slightly, but not significantly, more dissatisfaction. It is conjectural but perhaps the poor widows have accepted their circumstances, whereas their married counterparts expect and aspire to higher incomes given the support a spouse could provide, or need more income to maintain their larger households. The anomaly of well-off widows showing slightly more dissatisfaction may be only a shaky finding based on the small cell size or might reflect some strange aspiration among the few rich widows included in the group. In any case, the findings suggest that sheer income is a gross indicator of needs and desires, and we shall postpone any further discussion until we review table 2.4 which may clarify the findings. Similarly, no differences in satisfaction with health that might have been masked in the earlier analysis are unearthed when comparisons between the married and widowed are made at various levels of income.

Table 2.4 examines whether the effects of widowhood are intensified or weakened among those who bear the burdens children may create and experience the benefits they provide. Clearly, widows are less happy, find life less exciting, derive less satisfaction from family life than the married, no matter whether they have had many, few, or no children.[41] The chain of consequences that children create neither intensifies nor weakens the earlier findings. With respect to general happiness and excitement, perhaps children are a mixed blessing, the added burdens on the widow being offset by the psychic and, in some instances economic benefits derived from their presence. However, they are an unqualified blessing in one respect. Satisfaction with family life rises steadily and sharply when we compare widows with no, a few, and many children, although it never reaches the level of satisfaction among the married.

The presence or absence of children does not alter the earlier finding of very modest differences between the married and widowed in their satisfaction with finances. Although one would expect such dissatisfaction to be more acute when the widow has children she might still have to support and less acute when they already might contribute to her support, these influences seem to balance out in the net, and the earlier picture remains unchanged. It must be seen, of course, in the context of the ages of the children, that background noted earlier. However, satisfaction with health is contingent upon whether the widow has children. The earlier trivial difference between the married and the widowed becomes sharper in the subgroups with children. Why satisfaction declines under this condition is beyond the scope or power of our analysis.

In table 2.5 widows who live alone and widows who live with others (including but not limited to children) are compared to see whether physical isolation, rather than privation, mediates or modifies the earlier findings on effects. In

Table 2.4. The effects of widowhood as related to number of children (white women aged 40–79 in the 1972–78 surveys)

N =	No children[a] Married 129	No children[a] Widowed 71	One or two children[a] Married 583	One or two children[a] Widowed 181	Three or more children[a] Married 793	Three or more children[a] Widowed 212
Rating on happiness						
Very happy	50%	25%**	49%	22%***	42%	24%***
Not too happy	10	21	7	21	7	16
Life generally[b]						
Exciting	44	26**	40	32***	41	31*
Dull	1	13	3	13	3	9
Satisfaction with family life[c]						
Great deal or very great	79	49***	86	69***	86	72***
Little or none	1	23	1	3	0	3
Satisfaction with finances						
Not at all satisfied	13	10	11	16	17	21
Satisfaction with health[c]						
Great deal or very great	54	50	60	47*	57	44**
Little or none	5	6	6	7	6	13

*** Difference by two-tailed chi-square test significant at p ≤ 0.001.
** Difference significant at p ≤ 0.01 > 0.001.
* Difference significant at p ≤ 0.05.
a. Ever born, living or dead.
b. On this item, the Ns are reduced by about one-third.
c. On these items, the Ns are reduced by about 15 percent.

interpreting the findings, one should recall that widows who live alone are older. Such isolation does not significantly affect the feelings of widows, except in the area of satisfaction with finances where those who live with others are less satisfied. This may reflect, to some extent, simply the fact that they are the younger widows who, relative to others, are most deprived financially, as shown earlier. And because they are worse off, they may have found it necessary to move in with others. Thus the finding should not be taken to mean that physical isolation within the household has a salutary effect in raising such satisfaction. Despite this possible clarification of one paradoxical finding, it may still seem strange that physical isolation does not dampen happiness and excitement, or reduce satisfaction with family life. One might have expected those without companions or children in the household to be more lonely.[42] But here again one should recall the earlier findings that the widowed have heightened informal social relations of a variety of sorts which may compensate for the lack of companions at home. And the companions at home—often the children—are a responsibility that can be a source of worry as well as satisfaction. Indeed table 2.4 showed, with one exception, that whether a widow had children or not had little effect on her satisfaction.

Table 2.5. The effects of widowhood as related to living arrangements (white widows aged 40–79 in the 1972–78 surveys)

		Widows who live	
		Alone	With others
	N =	306	158
Rating on happiness			
Very happy		24%	22%
Not too happy		18	22
Life generally[a]			
Exciting		33	26
Dull		11	10
Satisfaction with family life[b]			
Great deal or very great		66	71
Little or none		8	2
Satisfaction with health[b]			
Great deal or very great		47	44
Little or none		9	11
Satisfaction with finances			
Not at all satisfied		14	25***

*** Difference significant at $p \leq 0.001$.
a. On this item, the Ns are reduced by about one-third.
b. On these items, the Ns are reduced by about 15 percent.

Effects as Related to Recency of Widowhood

The effects documented in these nationwide surveys are few in number and modest in magnitude. Even under conditions of privation and isolation, their magnitude is not extreme. Some might argue, however, that widowhood did have more massive effects that were dissipated by the time these measurements were made. They would emphasize the fact presented initially: only a small minority of the widows were in their first year of bereavement and, depending on their age, about half to two-thirds of the group had been widowed for more than five years. Even so, this would not weaken the force of the findings. The crucial questions neglected in past research and addressed in our study are whether there are long-lasting effects of various kinds, and their frequency in the general population.

Although the question on recency of widowhood was asked only in the two most recent surveys, it does open an avenue to obtain nationwide evidence on short-term effects.[43] Table 2.6 examines effects among widows contrasted in the recency of their bereavement. The size of the subgroups naturally is small compared to the numbers that were pooled over seven surveys, and the findings are therefore tentative. However, since short-term effects are important in terms of their practical and theoretical significance, the findings are worth presenting. Despite the numbers, they are based on unbiased, national samples. Other

Table 2.6. The effects of widowhood as related to recency of the experience (white widows aged 40–79 in the 1978 and 1980 surveys)

	Widowed within last 5 years	Widowed more than 5 years ago
N =	54	83
Rating on happiness		
Very happy	17%	21%
Not too happy	24	11
Life generally[a]		
Exciting	22	29
Dull	11	11
Satisfaction with family life		
Great deal or very great	67	74
Little or none	2	3
Satisfaction with health		
Great deal or very great	46	47
Little or none	11	11
Satisfaction with finances		
Not at all satisfied	30	22

a. Not asked in 1978; the Ns are reduced by about 50 percent.

findings based on two additional national samples, to be presented in chapter 3, will strenghten the conclusions about short-term effects.

The differences are small or negligible in all but the first test, the rating on happiness. Even there unhappiness is increased by only a modest amount among those recently bereaved. In light of past studies in the literature, the minimal short-term effects may seem surprising. Again, it should be stressed that those studies usually examined the immediate aftermath of widowhood. Most of the recently widowed examined in table 2.6 are past that stage, but it also should be stressed that the experience is not years behind them, and it is reasonable to regard it as recent.[44]

There is another possible explanation of the surprising finding. Those widowed long ago, naturally are a somewhat older group than those recently widowed. (Thus 86 percent of those long widowed are sixty or older whereas 74 percent of the recently widowed are sixty or older.) On variables where aging per se dampens bad effects, the two factors, age plus distance from bereavement, combine additively to make the results in the table more compelling. The differences between recently bereaved and young widows versus those widowed long ago and old should be sharpened. However, on some variables where being young would work in opposition to recency of widowhood, the effects would become obscured. Although the cells are small, the effects of recency were re-examined separately for younger widows (those under age sixty) and older widows (age sixty to seventy-nine). Only on the variable of happiness was the modest effect shown in table 2.6 greatly intensified. Among the young

Table 2.7. Comparisons of old and very old white widows (pooled data, NORC annual national surveys, 1972-78)

	Widows aged 80 or older	Widows 60-79
N =	109	346
Rating on happiness		
Very happy	29%	27%
Not too happy	17	17
Life generally[a]		
Exciting	30	31
Dull	7	12
Satisfaction with family life[b]		
Great deal or very great	61	68
Little or none	8	6
Satisfaction with health[b]		
Great deal or very great	37	43
Little or none	17	10
Satisfaction with finances		
Not at all satisfied	9	15

a. On this item, the Ns are reduced by about one-third.
b. On these items, the Ns are reduced by about 15 percent.

recently widowed, almost half fall in the bottom category reporting that they are "not too happy." Short-term emotional effects among young widows are severe! This specific finding is congruent with the literature; many past studies— as reviewed in chapter 1—explored only the immediate emotional aspects among young widows. However, the multiple tests in table 2.6 suggest that the effects of recency remain circumscribed and do not ramify into other areas.[45]

The Very Old Widows

Thus far the effects of widowhood have been found to be few in number and modest in magnitude among the old and the young, whether widowed recently or long ago, even among those living under conditions of privation or isolation. However extensive and penetrating the search has been up to now, it has stopped at age seventy-nine. What if we pushed beyond this point? Although past literature and our own evidence suggest that effects are more severe among young widows, we shall explore the problem among those eighty years of age or older. Table 2.7 presents selected findings for "very old" widows still within the reach of conventional surveys of the noninstitutionalized population and still able and willing to be interviewed. As a point of comparison, the earlier findings on the selected variables for the old widows, those aged sixty to seventy-nine, are also presented. (Both groups are purified, having no previous history of divorce or separation.)

The profiles of the very old and the old widows are almost identical, apart from the very small, perhaps trivial reduction in satisfaction with health and family that one might expect among the very old. Dissatisfaction with finances, it will be recalled, was muted among the old in contrast with the young widows. It is even less vocal among very old widows, and this despite the stark conditions under which they must be living. Their median annual income during those years was $3,142 as compared with $3,940 for widows age sixty to seventy-nine. In this renewed search, as before, we have failed to find severe social and psychological effects of widowhood.[46]

Conclusion

These many findings on the effects of widowhood were based on a quasi-experimental design containing a large number of cases drawn from seven carefully conducted national sample surveys. Three groups of widowed, married, and divorced or separated white women were purified and refined in various ways to achieve rigorous tests of the effects of widowhood; additional controls on age and other factors were introduced; then multiple comparisons on many social and psychological variables were made. The conclusions are clear and consistent. Nevertheless, let us withhold final judgment until we examine the findings in chapter 3. In contrast with the current cross-sectional findings, those additional findings directly trace effects of widowhood over time by a longitudinal design extracted from other carefully conducted national surveys.

3. Nationwide Longitudinal Surveys

The two surveys used in these analyses were conducted by the Survey Research Center of the University of Michigan (hereafter referred to as SRC). Like the NORC surveys, these involved a rigorous form of area-probability sampling of the noninstitutionalized, English-speaking, adult population of the continental United States.[1] Again, it would follow that all kinds of widows would be included in these samples in their proper proportions.[2] The SRC, like the NORC, is notable for the normally high quality of its sampling and other procedures, but these particular studies were part of a major, long-established program of research at the Center. Special care, senior personnel, and money were lavished on the surveys, and the continuation of the program over many years provided ample time to acquire experience and improve procedures. Admittedly, misfortune can strike the best surveys; errors can occur. The use of the two surveys is "double-insurance" against an accident, just as the use of seven surveys in the earlier analysis "overinsured" us.

The SRC surveys, unlike the NORC ones, are panel studies in which the same sample of respondents is reinterviewed, sometimes more than once, over a time interval to measure change or stability in a phenomenon and to analyze the causes. Panel studies of any kind are rare because of their cost and complexity. These two—covering the entire nation with large samples and spanning a four-year interval with three or more "waves" of interviewing—are rarer yet. They offered an invaluable opportunity, not previously exploited, to study widowhood longitudinally and to obtain generalizable, replicated evidence on its long- and short-term effects at little cost via secondary analysis.

The surveys focused on voting and other forms of political behavior, and waves of interviewing for the earlier panel were conducted around the 1956 and 1960 presidential elections, and in between during the 1958 off-year election; for the later panel around the 1972 and 1976 presidential elections, and during the off-year 1974 election.[3] As in the NORC surveys, many background characteristics—sex, age, race, income, size of household, number of children, and other features of the person's profile—were also measured for analytical reasons. And since marital status might have changed over time, SRC wisely, fortunately for us, measured that characteristic at least three times during the four-year span of each panel. This procedure was incidental to their goals, but crucial for our purposes. As a result, representative nationwide samples of those whose widowhood followed a particular pattern over time, for example, widowed on the first wave, widowed two years later, and still widowed four years later on the last wave, could be located and compared in many respects with others who exhibited a contrasted pattern of widowhood, for example, married on the initial wave but widowed by the last wave, and also compared with a representative sample of those who were and remained married over all waves of the panel or with those who were divorced throughout the four years.

Since the conceptualization of political behavior and its various social and psychological determinants was elaborate, the surveys happened to include a variety of variables relevant to appraising the effects of widowhood. Many had been measured repeatedly over the four years and change or stability in those respects could be examined.[4] Indeed the surveys contained such riches that we were able to explore all the areas previously examined in the NORC surveys except for health, and in one area explored not only the outlook on life and society but also the view of the self, and tested whether widowhood damaged self-regard.

What lay buried within each panel survey was a longitudinal study over a fairly long period of nationwide samples of the widowed of various types and of control groups of the married and divorced—simply waiting to be unearthed and exploited. By using the two panels, we gained not only the benefits of larger numbers and replication, but broadened the domain of effects examined, enlarged the array of measuring instruments on which the findings are based, and spanned the twenty-year period from the 1950s to the 1970s when historical changes might have modified the effects of widowhood. Although the repeated interviewing over the four-year course of the panels provides the opportunity for longitudinal study of the effects of widowhood, it also increases the risk of "survivor bias", the attrition of those most ravaged by time and widowhood. Therefore special attention was devoted to the problem and the new evidence, presented in a note because of its intricacy and length, coupled with the evidence presented earlier should allay concern.[5]

In theory, groups representing all the permutations of the pattern of widowhood—for example, those widowed in 1972 then remarried by 1974, then rewidowed by 1976; or those divorced in 1956 then remarried by 1958 and then widowed by 1960—could be included in the research design. But most of the patterns involving rapid change, because of its low incidence, are very rare in the general population and correspondingly in the samples. Many groups, however informative they might have been for the problem, had to be eliminated.

The final design included four groups: (1) those who were widowed on the first, middle, and last waves, labeled the *persistently widowed*, whose widowhood by the final wave had been prolonged for four more years; (2) the *persistently married*, married on all the waves whose marriages by the final wave had been prolonged by four more years; (3) the *divorced*, who were either divorced or separated on all the waves, that status by the final wave having been prolonged for four more years; (4) the *recently widowed*, composed of those who were married on the first wave but widowed by the middle and still on the final wave plus those who were married on both the first and middle waves but widowed by the final wave, all of the group having been widowed for less than four years. As noted later, depending on the panel about half to two-thirds of the "recent" group had been widowed for less than two years.[6]

The longitudinal comparisons of the four groups, as in the previous NORC analyses for the reasons then noted, have been restricted to white women. Thus sex and race are automatically controlled throughout and cannot account for any of the differences between groups.[7] And the initial difference in the age of the groups—persistently widowed being relatively old, persistently married and divorced relatively young, and recently widowed in between in age—also cannot confound the conclusions since age will be controlled during the analysis.

To summarize the design, four groups of white women: those widowed recently, those widowed relatively long ago, those with marriages of relatively long duration, and those with divorces of relatively long duration were measured repeatedly over four years. Age-controlled comparisons of the initial scores on a series of relevant variables and the later scores as the groups moved further on their contrasted courses will reveal the short- and long-term effects of widowhood. A change in score among one group of widows (for example, toward greater bitterness or sadness) by itself cannot be treated as an effect of the onset or prolongation of widowhood. Sheer aging of the group, and events other than widowhood might have produced the change. However, in contrast with case studies and surveys confined to widows, the multiple comparison or control groups in the design protect the conclusions. Since all the groups have aged and experienced the same flux of historical events, changes that are differential or distinctive in one or both groups of widows cannot be attributed to these other common factors. And one cannot rule out the possibility that the sheer process of repeated measurement in a longitudinal study limited to widows might artificially produce or reduce the changes in scores. Here again the multiple-group design provides protection since the other groups have also been repeatedly measured, and differential changes cannot be attributed to that constant factor.[8]

Although some features are common to all four groups, they also provide instructive contrasts. The married, of course, are like the conventional control group in an experiment, currently having no experience of widowhood and presumably none in the past. (Their past histories will soon come to light.) The recently widowed are like the conventional experimental group in a "before-and-after" design, examined prior to any exposure to widowhood and again shortly after the onset of the experience, or to put it another way when they have had only a small amount of exposure to widowhood. The persistently widowed represent the experimental group caught at a later point in time long after the onset of the experience or to put it another way when they have had cumulatively a larger amount of exposure to widowhood. And the divorced represent an unconventional comparison or control group. They are not exposed to widowhood but nevertheless have lost husbands. Their experience, as suggested in chapter 2, is qualitatively different in character and their inclusion in the study enriches the findings and clarifies the distinctive effects of widowhood. Other implications of the comparisons of the four groups and additional features of the quasi-experimental design will be reviewed later.

The research design imposed upon these panels would have come closer to the ideal if we had been able to screen out of the married and widowed groups, as in the NORC analysis, women with a history of divorce prior to the first wave of the panel. Then the contrasts between those groups and with the divorced or separated group would have been sharpened and the ambiguity previously noted, stemming from some people's definition of the term widowhood, would have been eliminated. We would then have a purer and more powerful test of the effects of widowhood. The appropriate screening question was not available in the SRC surveys and some individuals of a mixed type are contained within the two groups. However, the NORC screening which refers to the same population and time period as the 1970s panel suggests that the impurity would be no greater than 14 percent in that panel, and would be much less—about half that much—in the earlier panel.[9]

Similarly, it would have been ideal to screen out of the married and the divorced or separated groups those women with a history of widowhood prior to the first wave so as to sharpen the comparisons with the "widowed" group. Here again the NORC findings from the question in the 1978 and 1980 surveys yield an estimate of that kind of impurity that would be applicable to the 1970 panel. Among the currently married, 3–4 percent reported the death of a spouse in the past. Among the currently divorced or separated, 6–8 percent reported the death of a spouse. The latter figure may seem high but it does not mean that all of those individuals were in the strict sense of the term, previously widowed. From the nature of the question and in the light of the ambiguity stemming from people's concept of widowhood the figure should be regarded as a maximum estimate and probably is considerably overestimated.[10] This impurity in the two groups, at worst, is of small magnitude.

A sharp contrast between the recently and the persistently widowed would also be a desirable feature of the design. This, in fact, has been achieved. About two-thirds of the recent widows lost their spouses within the two years prior to the final wave of the panel, whereas the later discussion will show that about two-thirds of the persistently widowed had lost their spouses more than nine years prior to that point.

Fortunately, the imperfections in the research design do not spoil the rich inheritance that comes to us by way of secondary analysis. We must make the most of it, and now turn to the findings.

The Persistently Widowed

As a context for the later findings on the effects of widowhood, as before, we show in table 3.1 the contrasted profiles of "old" and "young" women who remained married or widowed throughout the course of the panel surveys. (The divorced group is omitted from the table but will be treated later on in the analysis.)[11] Again, the features are arranged under the three headings: personal characteristics, current milieu, and childhood milieu. In a single survey, naturally, the size of these groups is bound to be much smaller than the size built up by pooling seven NORC surveys, but by using two panels the evidence is buttressed and the numbers when combined are not insubstantial.

The fact that the data are based on panel surveys—repeated measurements of the individuals who were married at the time of the initial interview and still married when reinterviewed two and four years later, and of those persistently widowed—strengthens the evidence and also enlarges our knowledge. For objective characteristics known on logical or empirical grounds to show little or no true change over time (e.g., the educational attainments or the number of children middle-aged or older adults have) the panel data are a check on random errors of measurement, where the evidence to be presented will be comforting. For objective characteristics that might well change over time (e.g., size of household or income) the panel data reveal what happened to these women as they moved further along their contrasted courses of marriage or widowhood, where some of the evidence to be presented will be depressing.[12]

Again, as in the NORC data for the period 1972–78, a dramatic, statistically significant difference is documented by the very first item in the table. Among the old, median family income for 1971 of the married women is almost double that of the widowed, and it is more than double among the young. The 25th percentile of the distributions is also entered in the table and shows the depth of poverty within the lowest quarter of the widowed. That statistic vividly conveys the deprivation, especially of the younger ones, relative to their married counterparts. By 1975, average family income of the general population (in current, unadjusted dollars) had risen, so by then the young widows did have more dollars at their disposal. What should be noticed is the slow rise in their incomes. The gap between them and their married counterparts had not narrowed. Among the old, whether married or widowed, incomes tend to be fixed, and the figures show little change between 1971 and 1975. If anything, the gap between the two old groups had widened slightly by 1975. Clearly, the old widowed were severely deprived compared to their married counterparts at both points in time.

Confidence in these findings is enhanced by the close correspondence between the Michigan 1975 estimates and the NORC estimates (a running average based on the 1972–78 surveys, the mid-point being the 1975 survey). The incomes reported in 1956 in the earlier panel naturally were much lower in all of the groups, but the deprivation of widowhood again is dramatically documented. However, less weight should be given these findings since the question asked ("About what do you think your total income will be this year for yourself and your immediate family?") required considerable guesswork in contrast with the question about income already accrued in 1971 and 1975 asked of the panel in 1972 and 1976. That question was also far more detailed and comprehensive in specifying that the "figure should include dividends, interest, salaries, wages, pensions, and other income."

Table 3.1. The profiles of persistently widowed and married white women (SRC National Panel Surveys in the 1970s and 1950s)

	Old[a]		Young[a]	
	Married	Widowed	Married	Widowed
Personal characteristics				
Income				
1970s panel				
Total family income 1971				
(1972 interview)				
Median	$7068	$4100	$10940	$5160
25th percentile	3540	2080	8760	2460
Total family income 1975				
(1976 interview)				
Median	7570	4430	15705	6999
25th percentile	4950	2875	11810	4600
1950s panel				
Estimated 1956 total family income				
(1956 interview)				
Median	4440	1285	5857	3600
25th percentile	2770	579	4115	2500
Educational attainment				
1970s panel				
8th grade or less	36%	39%	12%	22%
9–12 grades	45	40	63	35
More than twelve	18	20	24	43
1950s panel				
1956 interview				
8th grade or less	29	57	29	27
9–12 grades	50	36	51	67
More than 12	21	7	21	7
1958 interview				
8th grade or less	29	56	29	21
9–12 grades	55	37	51	79
More than 12	16	7	20	0
Current religious affiliation[b]				
1970s panel				
Protestant	80	81	68	65
Catholic	15	14	29	26
Jewish	4	1	1	0
None	1	4	0	4
1950s panel				
Protestant	73	86	67	60
Catholic	21	9	26	33
Jewish	4	5	6	7
None	2	0	1	0

Table 3.1. (continued)

	Old[a]		Young[a]	
	Married	Widowed	Married	Widowed
Number of children (living or dead)[c]				
1970s panel				
1974 interview				
None	22%	14%	4%	13%
One	15	19	15	17
Two	31	19	25	30
Three or more	33	49	57	39
1976 interview				
None	18	14	4	13
One	14	17	15	22
Two	33	21	24	26
Three or more	36	48	58	39
Current milieu				
Household size				
1970s panel				
1972 interview				
One person	0	77	0	35
Two	89	11	30	48
Three or more	11	11	70	17
1976 interview				
One person	0	79	0	61
Two	95	11	38	26
Three or more	6	10	62	13
Household composition				
1970s panel				
No children in house age 5–18	98	93	40	78
Adults in household				
1950s panel				
1956 interview				
One	0	75	0	80
Two	93	14	87	20
Three or more	7	11	13	0
1958 interview				
One	0	75	0	60
Two	91	11	85	33
Three or more	9	14	16	7
Region living in currently				
1970s panel				
1972 interview[d]				
South	49	46	23	30
West	18	11	16	22
North	33	43	62	48
1976 interview				
South	49	46	24	30
West	18	11	16	22
North	33	43	60	48

Table 3.1. (continued)

	Old[a]		Young[a]	
	Married	Widowed	Married	Widowed
Childhood milieu				
Father's occupation during childhood				
1970s panel				
Professional or managerial	22%	21%	23%	18%
Farmer or farm laborer	39	50	30	50
Size of place raised in				
1970s panel				
Small town or rural area	75	83	65	60
1950s panel				
Small town or rural area	68	82	56	47
Ethnicity				
1970s panel				
Both parents born in U.S.	83	75	77	78
1950s panel				
Respondent born in U.S.	87	89	98	93

a. In the 1970s panel, the Ns are Old married—55, Young married—156, Old widowed—70, Young widowed—23. In the 1950s panel, the Ns are Old married—56, Young married—194, Old widowed—44, Young widowed—15. Depending on the characteristic, the bases used for the computation of percentages vary slightly because respondents occasionally gave no answer to one or another question. Whenever the number that had to be excluded were of more than trivial magnitude, it will be noted.

b. The percentages do not necessarily total 100 percent because a small number of respondents mentioned non-Christian or non-Jewish affiliations. The questions used to measure religious affiliation in the 1950s and 1970s panels differed in important respects, and therefore no strict comparison of the distributions derived from the two panels should be made, although comparisons of subgroups within each panel are legitimate. Because of the instruments used, one would also be tentative in any comparison of the NORC and SRC 1970s findings on religion.

c. Includes step-children and foster children.

d. South combines the SRC categories "solid South" and "Border States"; West combines "Mountain" and "Pacific" states; North combines New England, "Middle Atlantic," "East North Central," and "West North Central." For the definition of the original categories, see the SRC codebook.

For the reasons mentioned in chapter 2 the poverty, for the most part, should be seen as following widowhood rather than predating it. But additional evidence strengthens this inference. In exploring the psychological effects of widowhood, as already noted, we shall add to our design and analysis at a later point a third group, the "recently widowed:" those who were married when they were initially interviewed on the first wave of the panel but who had become widowed by the time they were interviewed on the final wave of the panel four years later. The size of that strategic group is very small, but nevertheless provides compelling evidence of the financial consequences that follow widowhood. Among the young members of this group the median income in 1971, when still married, was $11,000—almost matching to the dollar the median income of the young who were and remained married over the entire period, but far higher than the income of their counterparts who were already widowed at that point. By 1975, however, after their recent widowhood their median income was $10,500. Formerly equivalent to the married, they had fallen far below the figure of $15,705 that the married had reached in the interim, although they had not yet fallen as far as those long widowed, whose median income was only $6999 in 1975. Among the old members of the strategic group the median income in 1971, when still married, was $5999, considerably below that year's figure for their age counterparts who remained married throughout, but still above the figure for those already widowed. But by 1975 the median figure after their recent widowhood was $4,500, bringing them down far below the 1975 figure for the old who were still married and down to the level of those who had long been widowed. Thus, although the analysis of those strategic groups provides some additional evidence that those who are initially poor are at greater risk of becoming widowed, most of the evidence strengthens the conclusion that poverty follows widowhood.[13]

Other features of the profile of the persistently widowed, presented in table 3.1, are also revealing on this issue. There is certainly strong evidence from the repeated measurement in the 1956 panel that the widowed have lower educational attainment, suggesting that they came from less advantaged families.[14] Yet the evidence from the 1970 panel on education and on father's occupation does not suggest that their early origins were any lower than those who remained married. On the basis of the combined evidence, not consistent, remote in time and indirect in character, one would conclude that the initial handicap of widows was modest at most and that they became much poorer as a result of their widowhood.

One other feature of the profiles of the persistently married and widowed differs dramatically: their living arrangements. The panel findings in 1972 are almost identical with those from the NORC surveys in the 1970s. About three-quarters of the old widows live alone, while all of the married are living with others, mainly in two-person households. In both groups, given their advanced age, almost no young children (those age five to eighteen) are in the household when they do live with others. Among the younger women the same patterns are foreshadowed. About a third of the widows live alone, while none of the married live alone. The younger married are much more likely to be in three-person (or larger) households than the older married, the great majority of them having such living arrangements. By contrast, among the young widows who do not live alone, two-person households are the predominant pattern. And the composition of these households differs, young children being more common in the homes of the married young, although not the modal pattern.

In the 1950s panel the variable shown in the table is the number of adults in the household, rather than total persons, to supplement our knowledge of the details of the living arrangements. In the first wave of that panel, in 1956, three-quarters or more of the widows, whether young or old, lived in households containing no other adults. All of the married had other adults present, which would almost be true by definition except in those very rare instances where the husband is away for an extended period in military service, or on business, or in an institution.

The repeated measurement of these variables in later waves of both panels, four years later in the 1970s panel and two years later in the 1950s panel, reveals changes in household composition as the persistently married and widowed continue on their contrasted courses. Among the married, consistently and at both age levels, net change in household size is negligible despite the passage of two or four years. Among old widows, net change in the household is also negligible.[15] But quite dramatic changes in the distribution of household size ensued among the younger widows. The patterns of change are not consistent across both panels but this is not surprising. The 1970s variable, total size of household, includes children. Among younger widows, children might have grown up in the interim and left the household, it then shrinking in total size—the pattern observed in the 1970s data. The 1950s variable includes only adults and admits of many possibilities that might characterize the changing domestic arrangements of young widows. They might have taken in older widowed mothers or sisters no longer able to manage on their own, or themselves have found living alone too difficult and moved in with a grown child or sister. They might have taken a roommate or a lover, in these and other ways enlarging the household—the pattern observed in the 1950s data. And for all we know, widows' preference for various domestic arrangements may have changed historically in the eighteen-year period between the 1958 and 1976 measurements. Although we have not described the nature of the changes that did occur, the data establish that the domestic arrangements of younger white widows involve big changes over short periods of time.

Most widows have (or had) some children. However, as in the NORC data, younger widows are more likely than their married counterparts to have had small families or no children at all. In other respects the profiles of the persistently married and widowed are not markedly different. On many characteristics the groups show striking similarities. As noted earlier, living alone and poverty are the consequences of widowhood. Thus these may be links in a process that leads to more subtle social-psychological effects, but there is no need to control these variables in order to avoid spurious conclusions about the effects of widowhood. With table 3.1 in place and the context in mind, we turn to the effects revealed in the SRC panels.

Table 3.2 examines potential effects of widowhood by comparisons of those white women who remained persistently married or widowed over the four-year course of the panel surveys. Four of the same five areas of the broad domain already treated in the NORC analysis are again covered, health being the only area where the absence of questions in both panel studies prevents examination of such effects. Tests on many of the specific variables are replicated across the two panels, often by identical questions asked in both inquiries. Almost always several indicators and sometimes lengthy batteries of questions increase the reliability and comprehensiveness of the measurement of a variable and of the broad area being explored. Especially in the area labeled "Outlook" many more relevant and varied questions were available in the SRC panels than in the

NORC surveys. As before, all questions were chosen "blindly," before inspecting the cross-tabulations by marital status.

In a considerable number of instances, a question was asked on only one (not necessarily the first) wave of a panel. Then, of course, we cannot measure the changes that might occur as the widowed and married move further along in their contrasted careers. But such informative findings are included in the table since it would be negligent and profligate to ignore them. Although measurements based on repeating identical questions are lacking, one relevant measurement on nationwide samples representative of widowed and married white women was obtained. The SRC panels, under such conditions, have simply shrunk from longitudinal down to cross-sectional, one-time surveys equivalent in design to the NORC surveys whose value has already been documented. And where the single measurement refers to the same variable measured in the other panel or in the NORC surveys, which often used the identical questions, it provides a replication and can be used to test the stability and reliability of the findings.

There are other contrasted instances where the panels provide unusually lavish resources, where the same questions were used not just twice, but on all three waves of a panel.[16] These data show the changes that occur as the persistently widowed and married reach two points along the course, two years later and then four years later, and thus can reveal such subtle patterns of change as progressive worsening of the widow's morale with time, a decline in adjustment that is incipient and slow to set in, a temporary sharp decline followed by improvement or complete return to normalcy, or no change whatsoever over the shorter or longer run. These valuable data will not be wasted, but will only be treated in the text whenever they have something to contribute. As the reader will soon see, the presentation of two waves of data make table 3.2 intricate enough to follow, and including the three waves would overburden the table and the reader. Since the long-term effects of widowhood seem to us the crucial issue, the intermediate, second-wave data were omitted whenever the choice had to be made. Although the divorced are used in these analyses as a second comparison or control group, they will only be treated in the text since their inclusion in the table would also overburden it.

A few other remarks prefatory to table 3.2. Since widows as a group, obviously, are much older than the married, and since age itself might strongly influence outlook on or satisfaction with life, social involvement, and financial situation, controlling age in these comparisons is essential to prevent spurious conclusions about the effects of widowhood. The procedure employed is different from that used in the NORC analysis, but it controls age just as effectively and has the added advantage that it compresses the panel data, already unwieldy, for easier presentation in table 3.2. Instead of showing two sets of comparisons of married and widowed, one set for those who are young and a separate set for the old as in the earlier tables, and on top of that showing the changes in each group over the waves of the panel, we shall compare only the two aggregate groups:

widowed of all ages versus married of all ages. But age will be controlled by standardization, by combining the results obtained from the young and old married with appropriate weights to represent the findings that would have been obtained if the married had the same proportions of young and old as the widows. The procedure has a long history and legitimacy in the field of demography from which it was adapted successfully for survey analysis.[17] It exerts effective control over the initial age differences between widowed and married, and it simplifies the evaluation as well as the presentation of the findings. We must pay a small price for these benefits. Any effects of widowhood that are differential in the young versus the old are obscured in the aggregate findings in the table. However, since the separate findings for young and old were available and were examined in the process of standardization, any large differential effects that occurred will be reported in the text.

One other aid to the reader is included in table 3.2. The entries in the column labeled "Diff." show the magnitude of the net change that occurred over the waves of the panel as the persistently widowed and married moved along on their contrasted courses, and also the direction of that change. A plus sign denotes an improvement in morale or adjustment, greater psychic comfort, a more positive view of the self and the world with the passage of time; a minus sign, a change in the opposite direction. Some readers may say that our standard is too hedonistic in tone, that pleasure should not be the principle for evaluating the goodness of the change, that heightened sensitivity to the pain and harsh realities of widowhood with the passage of time would be a truer measure of "improvement." Then they can easily reverse the signs entered to suit their standards of judgment. Area I in table 3.2 corresponds to area I in table 2.2, and we turn now to those findings.

Feeling Tone

As would be expected on the basis of the literature and in light of the NORC findings, when asked in 1972 on the initial wave of measurement "How satisfying do you find the way you're spending your life these days?" the persistently widowed reported less satisfaction than the married. The picture remained unchanged and the contrast just as sharp four years later. But it is hardly the picture of gloom painted in past studies. Only a small minority of widows rate their lives as "not very satisfying," the bottom category of the three-point scale attached to the question, and, as the reader can infer from the table by simple subtraction, the substantial majority of widows describe their life as "pretty satisfying." To be sure, the difference between the widowed and married is much greater, and statistically significant, in the younger group, but even among young widows only a small minority describe life as not very satisfying, and dissatisfaction is a bit less frequent among them than among young divorced women. These findings are surprisingly mild in tone as were the NORC findings, both sets obtained in the 1970s.[18]

Table 3.2. The effects of widowhood revealed by repeated comparisons over time of persistently widowed and married white women (SRC National Panel Surveys in the 1970s and 1950s)

	Widowed over entire time[a]				Married over entire time[a,b]			
	72 (56)	74 (58)	76 (60)	Diff.	72 (56)	74 (58)	76 (80)	Diff.
	(all figures in percentages)							
I. Feeling tone								
Overall satisfaction (1970s)								
Life these days is								
Completely satisfying	20		20	0	30		28	−2
Not very satisfying	14		12	+2	5		3	+2
II. Outlook on the world and self								
Misanthropy scale (1970s)								
Can't be too careful dealing with people	57		58	−1	53		45	+8
People look out for themselves	46		46	0	37		41	−4
Most people take advantage	31		39	−8	32		32	0
Political efficacy scale								
Officials don't care about people like me								
1970s	59		67	−7	49		58	−9
1950s	43		38	+5	23		29	−6
Politics too complicated for person like me								
1970s	78		77	+1	84		74	+10
1950s	74		68	+6	65		63	+ 2
Political cynicism scale								
Can trust Washington to do what is right only some or none of time								
1970s	37		67	−30	45		72	−27
1950s		31				30		
Government wastes lots of tax money								
1970s	84		77	+7	78		87	−10
1950s		46				50		
Government run by big interests looking out for themselves (1970s)	57		79	−22	62		65	−3
Personal competence scale								
Not sure life works out way one wants								
1970s	60		59	+1	58		56	+2
1950s		66	68	−2		46	48	−2
Things come up that change one's planning ahead								
1970s	58		65	−7	46		51	−5
1950s		49	40	+9		41	28	+13
Life's too much a matter of luck to plan ahead								
1970s	41		45	−4	23		37	−14
Problems of life too big to run life way one wants								
1970s	33		35	−2	34		26	+8
Am kind of person who gets bad luck								
1950s		34	20	+14		23	19	+4
When people disagree wonder if I'm right								
1950s	62				67			
In an argument often give in								
1950s		88				77		

Table 3.2. (continued)

	Widowed over entire time[a]				Married over entire time[a,b]			
	72 (56)	74 (58)	76 (60)	Diff.	72 (56)	74 (58)	76 (80)	Diff.
	(all figures in percentages)							
Feel other people push me around								
1950s		9				4		
Prefer type of job where told what to do								
1950s		61				71		
On important decisions often have trouble making up my mind								
1950s		52				37		
Sometimes give up before finished on things I've started								
1950s		30				29		
Explanation of women's lower status								
Men born with more drive—disagree strongly								
1970s	21				19			
Women less reliable workers—disagree strongly								
1970s	31				16			
Qualified women suffer job discrimination—disagree strongly								
1970s	11				1			
Society discriminates against women—disagree strongly								
1970s	26				16			
III. Social involvement								
Follow governmental and public affairs "most of the time"								
1970s	39		47	+8	41		47	+6
Listened to presidential campaign on radio								
1950s	58		41	−17	54		44	−10
Watched presidential campaign on TV								
1950s	69		78	+9	81		90	+9
Read about presidential campaign in newspaper								
1950s	74		77	+3	75		84	+9
Read about presidential campaign in magazines								
1950s	26		30	+4	39		46	+7
Watch evening national TV news—frequently								
1970s		77	76	−1		72	74	+2
Read a daily newspaper								
1970s		77	72	−5		83	83	0
Watch daytime TV entertainment shows—frequently								
1970s		33	29	+4		21	23	−2
Attend religious services								
1970s								
Never		11	13	−2		11	17	−6
Every week		41	35	−6		46	39	−7

Table 3.2. (continued)

	Widowed over entire time[a]				Married over entire time[a,b]			
	72 (56)	74 (58)	76 (60)	Diff.	72 (56)	74 (58)	76 (80)	Diff.
	(all figures in percentages)							
Number of voluntary association memberships								
1970s								
Zero	27				19			
One	31				32			
Two or more	41				49			
IV. Financial situation								
1970s								
Better off than before		10	12	+2		13	20	+7
Worse off		36	22	+14		31	18	+13
1950s								
Better off than before	19		13	−6	33		22	−11
Worse off	36		29	+7	17		18	−1
1970s								
Expect next year to be								
Better		3	16	+13		8	8	0
Worse		31	14	+17		27	12	+15
Satisfaction with present financial situation								
1950s								
Pretty well satisfied	43		48	+5	52		48	−4
Not satisfied at all	16		23	−7	9		14	−5
Satisfaction with present income								
1970s								
Delighted or pleased	24				24			
Unhappy or terribly unhappy	14				7			
Satisfaction with present standard of living								
1970s								
Delighted or pleased	37				35			
Unhappy or terribly unhappy	8				3			

a. In the 1970s panel, the Ns are Married over entire time—211; Widowed over entire time—93. In the 1950s panel, the Ns are Married over entire time—250; Widowed over entire time—59. Depending on the characteristic, the bases used for the computation of percentages vary slightly because respondents occasionally gave no answer to one or another question. Whenever the number that had to be excluded were of more than trivial magnitude, it will be noted.

b. Percentages shown for those married over entire time are standardized in terms of the age distribution of those widowed over entire time.

Outlook on the World and the Self

The first entries in this area are based on the same three-item "Misanthropy" scale used earlier in the NORC analysis where we had found, at most, one shred of evidence that the widowed in the 1970s were more misanthropic. The new analysis again provides, at most, a scintilla of evidence that the widowed are more misanthropic. On the first wave in 1972, the differences between widowed and married are negligible on two items; on the third item misanthropy is a bit more frequent among the widowed. Four years later, the widowed have become a bit more sour on one item whereas the married have become a bit sweeter on another. As a result of the changes the widowed end up somewhat more misanthropic, but the small differences on two of the three items at that end point do not warrant the conclusion that embitterment distinctively characterizes the persistently widowed.[19] Examination of the separate findings for young versus old widows does not alter the general conclusion.

The next two items in the table are from the longer, well-known scale SRC has used to measure "political efficacy," and were chosen "blindly" but because of their contrasted content. In the first item the person blames others for his lack of efficacy, and thus its content overlaps the "political cynicism" scale to which we will turn shortly and also partially overlaps the misanthropy scale. However, the bitterness towards others in the instance of misanthropy is focused on the mass of people, whereas now it is focussed specifically on the political elite. In the second item blame for any lack of efficacy is directed at the self, although the personal limitations explicitly acknowledged are specifically restricted to the political sphere. Thus the content partially overlaps the scale of "personal competence" to which we will turn later, although the lack of self-regard measured there is much more diffuse and encompassing in character. To some extent, therefore, various later findings will replicate these two tests.

Both the efficacy items were asked on the first and last waves of each panel, and what is revealed to us in that attractive design is a most interesting, if intricate pattern. In the 1950s and again in the 1970s the difference between widowed and married in political efficacy stemming from a sense of personal incompetence is negligible or not consistent on the first and last waves and the change over the four year periods is also negligible. Although the great majority of these women, whether married or single and whether drawn from the 1950s or the 1970s had little regard for themselves in this sphere, clearly widowhood had no effect.

On the other efficacy item, where the blame is put upon "public officials" for not caring "much what people like me think", a radical decline in efficacy of the same magnitude occurred within both the married and widowed groups between the 1950s and the 1970s and each group added on still another quantum of cynicism between 1972 and 1976. We should digress for a moment and contemplate the false conclusion that might have been drawn in a longitudinal study lacking any comparison with the married which tracked only the widows over the twenty years from 1956 to 1976, or just from 1972 to 1976. The data reveal simply the documented, understandable, secular trend toward the belief that our officials are uncaring.[20] But another subtle pattern can be seen. On the initial wave as well as the final wave of each panel, widows are somewhat more likely than the married to believe that officials don't care about people "like me," but that belief is not aggravated as their widowhood progresses. This seems to be one effect of widowhood, perhaps derived from and justified by the intractable fact (vividly documented in table 3.1) of their relative deprivation fro.   50s through the 1970s about which they may have expected more concern in officials. Considering the modest magnitude of the effect and the fact that it is based on only a single question, let us treat the conclusion as tentative until we examine the next set of findings on the three items drawn from the Michigan "political cynicism" scale.[21]

Although a measurement of change was not available for the 1950s panel on the first of these items, trust in the moral integrity of the "government in Washington," it is informative to find that there is no difference in the cynicism expressed in 1958 by the widowed and the married. Again in the 1970s we find a negligible difference in the cynicism of the two groups when they are measured on the first wave in 1972, and also on the final wave in 1976.[22] Indeed, the persistently widowed had become much more cynical about moral integrity in Washington, but so, too, had the married, and the change therefore is simply the pervasive decline in trust that had set in during the four-year interval. The findings are confirmed still another time, the question having been asked on the middle wave of that panel in 1974, when once again (though not shown) there was no difference between the widowed and the married. That measurement, however, does pinpoint the fact that the pervasive decline in trust had occurred between 1972 and 1974. Examination of the separate findings for young versus old reveals no consistent pattern over the two panels and the various waves of measurement nor any significant differences, and does not alter the general conclusions.

On the second of these items, again we find in the 1950s that the widows and married do not differ in cynicism implied in the belief that the government wastes a "lot of money we pay in taxes." Such cynicism increased radically by 1972 in both groups, the widows slightly more prone to it than the married. But by the 1976 wave, their positions reverse and the married express it more frequently. Clearly, there is no evidence that widowhood increases this aspect of political cynicism. If anything, the widows become slightly less cynical with the passage of time and events and the prolongation of their widowhood, while the married have grown more cynical. Here, too, the middle wave in 1974 confirms the picture, the two groups differing not at all. Separate comparisons among the young and old show no consistent differences.

On the third of these items asked in the 1970s "Would you say the government is pretty much run by a few big interests looking out for themselves or that it is run for the benefit of all the people," there is a dramatic effect, in contrast to the findings on the other two items.[23] Although the widows are a bit less cynical than the married group on the first wave of measurement (the difference hardly deserves notice), by 1976 when they have experienced four more years of widowhood, cynicism has become pervasive and far more widespread among them than among the married, who remained unchanged over the period.

The findings over these three questions and the earlier, relevant item from the political efficacy scale show that whatever effect widowhood may have in this sphere, it does not lead to a diffuse cynicism, a generalized bitterness toward government, but, at most, to a rather narrow and specific form. One may venture a tentative conclusion as to that form on the basis of the special content of the two items showing some effects. On the earlier items widows expressed the belief that government did not care about people "like me"; on the later item, they expressed the belief that government was not run "for the benefit of all the people." All the people is, indeed, a far more inclusive phrase, but it also includes the widows. The political cynicism of the persistently widowed relates specifically to government neglect, not to wastefulness or immorality, a sin of omission rather than commission in connection with their problems. Some additional evidence to be presented later will tell us whether these speculations are worth pursuing.

The next twelve items in the table examine the constellation labeled "personal competence" by the SRC investigators.[24] They describe the concept and its implications: it is "a feeling of mastery over the self and the environment. The person lacking such a sense of mastery may either be tense and anxious about the course of his personal life, or may be resigned in a fatalistic way to a succession of events with which he does not feel he can cope adequately." From considerable methodological research and extensive use of the scale in their panel and other surveys, they accumulated a good deal of evidence of the validity and reliability of the instrument and of its sensitivity in discriminating between contrasted groups. For example, individuals who scored low on competence gave responses to TAT pictures "which reflected a posture of an oppressive uncontrollable external reality" (Robinson, et al., 1969: 102–3). It is a plausible hypothesis that the trauma of widowhood and its prolongation would alter the view of the self and the world in ways that impair competence. We shall review the voluminous findings in somewhat omnibus fashion, since subsets have a common implication and the discrete findings from each item are presented to the reader for detailed examination.

On the first five items, all tapping a fatalistic view of the world with a pessimistic tint, we have measures of change from at least two waves of one of the panels. The four items in the 1970s panel were asked on all three waves, and on two of these we also have a replication from the 1950s. All five items were couched with explicit alternatives, although only the fatalistic, darker response is shown in the table.

This set of data certainly yields substantial evidence on the hypothesis. Although there are some exceptions (for example on the first item in the 1970s), the weight of the evidence suggests that widowhood does increase fatalism, a sense that life itself is beyond one's personal competence to control. The differences between the widows and the married are not great in magnitude, and are absent on some tests, but they are substantial and frequent enough to be noticed. As one examines the pattern over time, one also notes that the effect is not the end product of the prolongation of their widowhood. The difference can already be observed at whatever initial point a measurement is available to us.

Since this comparison is based on only the persistently widowed, already fairly far along on their course when they were first included in these surveys, we cannot yet locate the onset of the effect. The issue may be clarified by the data to be presented later. The intermediate wave findings are consistent with our general conclusions.

The next four items are along another dimension of the constellation. They refer to competence or mastery in dealing with others, rather than dealing with life itself. Although available from only one wave of the 1950 panel, the findings are clear and informative. (Again only the attribute indicative of incompetence is tabled; the alternative attribute is easily inferred.) There is no consistent evidence that widowhood produces any such impairment of the self. When we juxtapose the two sets of findings we see the underlying rationality. After all widows are expert witnesses to life's unpredictability, to what Sumner long ago termed its *aleatory element*. He suggested that good fortune is taken for granted, but that "the minds of men always dwell more on bad luck. . . . Misfortunes arrest their attention and remain in their memory" (Sumner 1913: 6). His observation would apply equally well to widows who would remember that they are in submission to life itself, to the uncontrollable and nasty turns it takes. But, clearly, they have not submitted to others. There they assert a sense of competence or mastery equal to that of the married.

The last two items on competence, available on only one wave of the 1950s panel, fall along a third dimension of the constellation. Without specifying the obstacles (by implication internal in character) the questions refer to competence or mastery in achieving one's goals. Taken together, they yield no consistent evidence that widowhood damages this aspect of personal competence.

The final set of four items under area IV of the table deal with a new variable. They were prefaced by a statement about the lesser achievements of women in our society, and the respondents were then asked whether they agreed with various explanations of that situation provided in the questions that followed. We chose two pairs of items from the longer battery. One pair placed the blame on others, locating the source of the disadvantage in discrimination, and the other blamed women themselves for their difficulties. The hypothesis that seemed plausible on a number of grounds was that widows would have become sensitive to discrimination. Their needs might have led them into the job market where they might have experienced discrimination and felt it acutely because of their circumstances. They might have developed a less "traditional" outlook because they were no longer under the influence of a husband or no longer concerned about competition he faced from women workers. Blaming others or the institutions of society might also reflect the (putative) bitter outlook they had developed toward the world. In contrast with the other effects examined, all of which focused on the destructive consequences of widowhood, these items focus on positive or functional consequences of widowhood, and thus produce a more balanced overall appraisal. Some might entertain an opposing hypothesis: that the possible damage to self-regard widows sustained might make them blame the disadvantage on themselves, on womankind. In any case, the items seemed promising.

On the one pair of items the "agree" response was associated with a "tradition-al" explanation, and on the other pair with an explanation in terms of discrimi-nation. Thus any acquiescence response-set, any tendency toward agreeing to whatever proposition is presented whatever its content is balanced out over the battery, and that source of error should not cloud the results. There is no evidence that widowhood has any consistent effect. The first item shows no difference. On the second widows are more likely to oppose a traditional expla-nation for the disadvantage of women, but on the third and fourth items widows are more likely to reject discrimination as the source of the disadvan-tage.[25] Examination of the separate findings at younger versus older age levels does not change the picture, although one might have expected more effect among younger widows because of their greater involvement in the labor mar-ket. It should be noted, however, that young divorced women are more likely than their married and widowed counterparts to oppose traditionalist views and to see discrimination as the source of the problem.

Social Involvement

Area III of table 3.2 shows the social involvement of those who were persist-ently widowed and married over the course of the panels. Some of the same variables, church attendance and media behavior, that were used in the earlier NORC analysis are examined once again, but the dimension of change can now be incorporated into the analysis as a result of repeated measurements.

The first of these items examines involvement in the wider world of politics. All the waves of these panels occurred during national elections (political behav-ior being the focus of the original inquiries), an unusually intense period. However, the question on all waves was prefaced by the statement "Some people seem to follow what's going on in government and public affairs most of the time, *whether there's an election going on or not*. Others aren't that inter-ested" (italics supplied), thus suggesting that the respondent abstract herself from the temporary context before answering. Whether we examine the first or the final wave, no differences between widowed and married are found, and the widows show no decline in involvement despite the prolongation of their state.[26] Examining the separate patterns at the two age levels reveals a substantially higher level of involvement among the young widows than among their married counterparts, certainly underscoring the conclusion that widowhood has no deleterious effect on this form of involvement. By contrast the young divorced show substantially less involvement than their married or widowed counterparts.

The next four items use media behavior as an index of social involvement as in the NORC analysis and for the reasons reviewed earlier, although the expo-sure now is in the context of presidential elections and refers specifically to political content. Widows and married were equally involved, as shown by their radio listening on both waves in the 1950s. We may digress to point the object lesson implicit in those findings. If we had conducted a longitudinal study of widows between 1952 and 1956, without benefit of a control or comparison group, we might have drawn the false conclusion from examining this variable that political involvement declined with the prolongation of widowhood. That decline characterized the married as well as the widowed and reflected the growth of television, exposure to which is examined next in the table. By this new indicator widows consistently show less involvement on both waves of measurement. The magnitude of the difference, however, is not marked, and examination of the differential findings at the two age levels shows that the effect is located exclusively among the old widows. A parsimonious possible explanation of this unusual finding is presented in the notes.[27]

The next two items use exposure to political content in printed media during the presidential campaigns of 1956 and 1960 as indicators of involvement. The pair of findings are not consistent. The one item, reading such magazine content, reveals considerably less exposure among the widows on both waves, again located exclusively among the older group. We shall also reserve for the notes a possible explanation of these findings which would discount their importance.[28]

The next three items on media exposure in the 1970s are couched broadly, not restricted to political content, and thus can be construed as indicators of involvement in the wider social world. Admittedly, the measurements were taken during political campaigns, but by using the 1974 wave data at least one of the measures is removed from the most heated context, and, of course, both groups were compared under the same heated conditions. On both waves, there are no differences in viewing evening TV news.[29] On one of the two waves widows report considerably less daily newspaper reading. This pattern is located mainly among the older widows, replicating the earlier NORC findings, and consistent with the SRC findings just reviewed above and in note 28 on exposure to political content in magazines and newspapers. In contrast with these findings, the young divorced are much less likely to be frequent watchers of TV evening news or readers of the daily papers.

The next item, frequent watching of daytime entertainment shows on TV, was examined as a possible indicator of tendencies toward escape from real social life. Weighing the findings in that light—perhaps giving them too much weight—widowhood increases such behavior by, at most, a modest amount.

Comparisons of the social and spiritual involvement indicated by frequency of attendance at religious services reveal no difference between the persistently widowed and married. The finding holds whether they are measured on the first wave of the 1970s panel or four years later or on the intermediate wave (although that datum is not tabled).[30] Widows are no more likely to reject formal religion or to seek the solace and social benefits such participation provides. The three waves show no consistent differential pattern at younger and older age levels, in contrast with the earlier NORC findings. Among the divorced, however, the pattern of "never" attending is far more prevalent than among either the married or the widowed, and the finding is consistent on all three waves of the panel, thus confirming the earlier NORC analysis.

The last item shown in section III of the table, membership in voluntary associations, confirms the earlier NORC finding. Widows are less likely to have social involvements of this formal type. In contrast with the NORC finding the pattern characterizes older as well as younger widows, but the difference between them and their married counterparts is of small magnitude.

Financial Situation

In section IV of table 3.2, as in the earlier NORC analysis, the psychological effect of the financial circumstances of widowhood is examined. Once again, the proper way to begin is to recall the objective facts presented in table 3.1. Median annual income of the persistently widowed was exceedingly low, and far below that of married women. The disparity was there in the cohort studied in the 1950s; it still existed in 1971 in the cohort of widows examined at that point, whose plight continued when their incomes were measured again four years later.

The situation was bad. It would be bad enough if it had remained the same for all of them, but as the first items in this section of table 3.2 show, a substantial minority reported for the current period that they were "worse off financially than . . . a year ago." They rendered that judgment repeatedly, on an early wave and on a later wave both in the 1950s and the 1970s panels.[31] Only much smaller minorities reported their current situation had improved, the majority of the persistently widowed judging their current situation as no better, no worse. Judgments that their financial situation had improved are more frequent among the married on both waves of both panels, although such judgments are not the modal response.

The poet claims that "hope springs eternal in the human breast," but as the data from an additional question asked repeatedly in the 1970s show, only a small minority of the persistently widowed "think that a year from now" they "will be better off financially." The majority—widowed and married alike—see their future finances as unchanging.

In light of the objective facts and these judgments, the way the persistently widowed respond to their circumstances, shown in the next items in table 3.2, is surely paradoxical. When asked in the 1950s, "Would you say that you are pretty well satisfied with your present financial situation, more or less satisfied, or not satisfied at all?" close to a majority say "pretty well satisfied," and only a small minority say they are "not satisfied at all," and there is little difference between them and the married. The finding is almost identical on repeated measurement. The nature of the questions asked in the 1970s panel makes the finding even more paradoxical and dramatic. After being asked: "How satisfied are you with the income you and your family have?" the respondents were presented with a seven-point scale ranging from "delighted" and "pleased" at one end down to "unhappy" and "terrible" at the other end. About a quarter of the persistently widowed describe themselves as either delighted or pleased with their income and only a very small minority are unhappy or terribly unhappy. They are almost as satisfied as the married.

Since income itself does not completely determine one's circumstances, the results from a second question in the 1970 panel provide even more compelling findings. When asked "How satisfied are you with your standard of living—the things you have like housing, car, recreation, and the like?" about a third of the persistently widowed express delight or pleasure and only a negligible number say they are unhappy or terribly unhappy. They hardly differ from the married in such satisfaction. In contrast with the NORC analysis, which found significantly more dissatisfaction (not that it was much in magnitude) among the young widows than among their married counterparts, the pattern is the same for both young and old in the SRC panels. By contrast, the young divorced are much more likely to express themselves as unhappy or terribly unhappy with their incomes and their standard of living than their widowed or married counterparts (as was true in the NORC analysis) despite the ironic fact that their actual incomes were somewhat higher than the widowed although considerably below that of the married.

In pondering the paradox, the reader's thought might have turned to the "rich widow." Table 3.1 reported only the median income of widows plus the 25th percentile of the distribution to show the poverty in the bottom quarter of the group. After all there are some rich widows, and it might be they who reported their delight or satisfaction. There are not enough of them to resolve the paradox. In 1971, 90 percent of the old widowed had incomes below $10,550; among young widows 90 percent fell below $11,350. Yet one quarter of all our widows were delighted or pleased and almost half checked "mostly satisfied."

What will resolve the paradox remains to be determined. Some relevant data and speculations will be presented later. Again, one thing should be stressed. These findings, however valid they are psychologically, do not validate the moral position that since the problem is accepted, nothing should be done to alleviate it. And although the day had not yet dawned in our data when dissatisfaction was prevalent, the day may not be far off when grievance spreads among the widows. The earlier findings that widows believed government was uncaring and neglectful of their interests may be intimations of what lies ahead.

Answers to another battery of questions asked of the 1970 panel are also signs of possible future grievances, although they had barely taken form among the widows in 1974. The respondents were first asked: "What are some of the problems that you face these days in your life?" Both younger and older widows were somewhat more likely than the married to say that they had no problems, that response characterizing about 20 percent of the widows. Even more surprising are the contrasts in the kinds of problems mentioned first by the groups.

The biggest problem for everyone was economic in nature but the married felt more oppressed, 53 percent of young married mentioning such problems, whereas 35 percent of young widowed mentioned them. Among the old, the respective figures were 42 percent and 31 percent. The next biggest class of problems related to health, and here the pattern was reversed. Among the young, 8 percent of the married and 17 percent of the widowed mentioned health. Among the old, however, there were no differences in reference to health, 21 percent of married and widowed mentioning it as their first problem.

When they were asked the same question again in 1976, the similarity in the findings is striking. Everyone's biggest problem was still economic. Among the young, 55 percent of the married mentioned that first against 38 percent of the widowed. Among the old, the respective figures were 38 percent and 30 percent. Health again came next. As before, among the young, 8 percent of the married mentioned it first against 19 percent of the widowed. Among the old, 26 percent of the married and 21 percent of the widowed mentioned health as their primary problem—a negligible difference. Among the old, widows were much more likely to say they had no problems, that response characterizing 26 percent of them in contrast with 13 percent of the married. However, among the young, in contrast with the 1974 finding, there was no difference in reported freedom from problems, 14 percent of the widowed and 13 percent of the married saying "no problems."

Then in 1974 they were asked in relation to the first or most important problem they had mentioned whether it "is something you have to work out on your own, or is there someone who ought to be helping?" Among the persistently widowed 49 percent said someone should be helping, and the standardized percentage among the married was a bit lower, 42 percent. When then asked whether the help should come from a private individual or agency, or a governmental agency, 73 percent and 74 percent of the persistently married and widowed respectively stated that the help should come from the government. Although no different in that respect, when asked to rate "how helpful do you feel the government is being?" a difference that parallels our earlier findings begins to emerge. Among the persistently married, 6 percent say "very helpful" and 59 percent "not helpful at all." However, not even one widow (0 percent) said the government has been very helpful and 61 percent said "not helpful at all."

The effects of widowhood traced through the two SRC panel studies are few and modest in magnitude. This overall conclusion is consistent with the earlier findings from the seven NORC surveys. But it is more striking and surprising since the domain explored is broader and we were able to penetrate deeper into it by repeated measurements of the widowed and married as they moved further along on their contrasted courses.[32] Yet these effects were explored only among the persistently widowed, all of whom had been widowed for more than four years by the time they were measured on the final wave of the panels. And although no direct measurement is available on exactly how long before the first wave of the panels they had become widowed, by applying the findings from the NORC question asked of equivalent samples in 1978 and 1980 with appropriate adjustment, one can derive the reasonable estimate that 62 percent of them had been widowed for more than five years on the first wave of the panels.[33] Thus on the final wave of measurement, the majority would have been at least nine years into their widowhood. Some might react in the same way as they did to the NORC findings, theorizing that widowhood does have massive traumatic effects but that by the time of our initial observations, and for sure our final observations, those effects were long since dissipated. Even if that were true, the findings bear on the crucial questions of whether there are long-lasting effects of various kinds, and their frequency in the general population of widows.

In evaluating the theory of short-term, transient effects, one should not neglect the fact that the first-wave measurements capture the persistently widowed at an earlier stage in their widowhood than the third-wave measurements. If there were merit to the theory, one would expect the differences between the married and widowed to be greater on the first wave than on the third wave, and the persistently widowed to exhibit more negative characteristics on the first wave than they do on the third wave. Re-examination of table 3.2 reveals no such regular pattern to the findings and should make such theorists pause. (The same logic would apply to the second- versus the third-wave findings which show no such progression.) To be sure, the traumatic effects of widowhood need not necessarily follow a linear path. They might appear in the very earliest stage and diminish quickly or disappear, the pattern thereafter remaining unchanged from the first through the last wave of our measurements. For the moment, the issue is still unresolved.

The Recently Widowed

Short-term, transient effects of widowhood, of course, are important. Until they are dissipated, they can cause havoc. They deserve documentation, attention, and amelioration. Given the methodological deficiencies of much past research on short-term effects and the limited generalizability of the findings, new explorations into such effects are especially important. As in the NORC national samples, the recently widowed drawn from these nationwide panels— those still married on the first wave but widowed by the last wave—are the vehicle needed for such explorations. This strategic group is very small in size because of the very low incidence of new widows in the general population over a short interval. One must treat the conclusions tentatively and not give undue importance to an occasional aberrant datum. However, since we rely on two such groups (in addition to the NORC group) drawn in unbiased fashion from the well-designed samples used in the 1950s and 1970s panel surveys, and a multiplicity of tests, the findings are strengthened to some degree.

Table 3.3 shows the effects that occurred among the recently widowed for all the variables where we had both first-wave measurements when they were still married and last-wave measurements four years later when all had become widowed. The intermediate wave of the panels when marital status was determined enables us to narrow down the recency of their widowhood. In the group from the 1970s, almost half had been widowed less than two years when they were measured on the final wave. In the group from the 1950s, almost two-thirds had been widowed less than two years when the final measurements were made. Certainly widowhood was recent enough for many, perhaps all of them to reveal effects other than purely fleeting ones.

The table also presents first- and last-wave measurements and patterns of change for the persistently married and widowed who serve in this analysis as essential comparison or control groups to isolate net effects of recent widowhood. As before, the percentages for the persistently married and the recently widowed are standardized in terms of the age distribution of the persistently widowed to control the age differences among the three groups; the persistently married being predominantly young, the persistently widowed being predominantly old, and the recently widowed falling in between in terms of age.[34]

The obvious thought as one approaches the table is that the recently widowed will resemble the persistently married on the first wave of measurement, but, on variables where we had previously observed long-lasting effects, will show the pattern of the persistently widowed on the final wave in incipient or aggravated form. And if one is guided by the theory of short-term, transient effects on variables where no long-term effects had been previously documented, one would expect the third-wave pattern of the recently widowed to differ from the patterns of both the persistently married and widowed in an undesirable direction. Such thoughts, however, are facile and may be too hasty. Consider other possible patterns.

Some of the recently widowed—perhaps many among the minority whose widowhood was more than two years in duration—were living with a terminally ill husband at the time of the first wave. The high cost and the uncertainty of how long it would have to be sustained, the time consumed and the burden in caring for so sick a person, plus the painfulness of the experience all could have powerful negative effects revealed on the first wave measurement. In these cases, how much worse can the situation get after widowhood? Indeed, the actual widowhood, by releasing them from such problems might temporarily have improved their scores on the final wave, the recently widowed not yet confronting a new set of nagging problems of prolonged widowhood.[35] Moreover, during the last phase of their marriages and the protracted illnesses of their husbands some of the recently widowed may have been or felt neglected and mistreated by others: employers and insurers who terminated benefits, friends and neighbors who wearied of helping month after month or found themselves ineffectual. Consequently, embitterment and other negative feelings may appear on the first wave. But then in the early stage of widowhood friends and relatives and neighbors might rally—if only for a short time, and new

Table 3.3. The effects of widowhood revealed by repeated comparisons over time of recently widowed with persistently widowed and married white women (SRC National Panel Surveys in the 1970s and 1950s)

	Married over entire time[a,b]			Recently widowed[a,b]			Widowed over entire time[a]		
	Time 1	4 yrs. later	Diff.	Married time 1	Widowed 4 yrs. later	Diff.	Time 1	4 yrs. later	Diff.
I. Feeling tone									
Overall satisfaction (1970s)									
Life these days is									
Completely satisfying	31%	27%	−4	30%	15%	−15	20%	19%	−1
Not very satisfying	5	3	+2	13	6	+ 7	15	12	+3
II. Outlook									
Personal competence scale (1970s)									
Not sure life works out way one wants	57%	55%	+ 2	79%	95%	−16	60%	59%	+1
Things come up that change one's planning ahead	45	50	− 5	40	49	− 9	58	63	−5
Life too much matter of luck to plan ahead	23	36	−13	17	49	−32	40	44	−4
Problems of life too big to run life way one wants	34	25	+ 9	27	27	0	32	34	−2
Political scale									
Officials don't care about people like me									
1970s	49	59	−10	43	52	−9	59	66	−7
1950s	23	28	− 5	31	25	+6	43	38	+5
Politics too complicated for person like me									
1970s	84	75	+9	59	67	−8	78	76	+2
1950s	64	63	+1	56	63	−7	74	68	+6

Table 3.3. (continued)

	Married over entire time[a,b]			Recently widowed[a,b]			Widowed over entire time[a]		
					Widowed				
	Time 1	4 yrs. later	Diff.	Married time 1	4 yrs. later	Diff.	Time 1	4 yrs. later	Diff.
Political cynicism scale (1970s)									
Can trust Washington government to do what is right only some or none of the time	44%	71%	−27	69%	73%	−4	36%	65%	−29
Government wastes a lot of our tax money	75	85	−10	69	46	+23	83	76	+7
Government run for few big interests	63	66	−3	54	43	+11	55	78	−23
Misanthropy scale (1970s)									
Can't be too careful dealing with people	53	45	+8	64	53	+11	57	58	−1
People look out for themselves	38	41	−3	46	61	−15	47	46	+1
Most people take advantage	33	32	+1	31	17	+14	30	39	−9
III. Social involvement									
Attend religious services (1970s)									
Never	11%	16%	−5	0%	8%	−8	11%	13%	−2
Every week	44	38	−6	31	30	−1	42	35	−7
Listened to presidential campaign on radio (1950s)	54	44	−10	44	37	−7	58	41	−17
Watched presidential campaign on TV (1950s)	81	90	+9	69	87	+18	69	78	+9
Read about presidential campaign in magazines (1950s)	38	46	+8	25	31	+6	26	30	+4
Follow governmental and public affairs "most of the time" (1970s)	41	47	+6	50	49	−1	39	47	+8

Table 3.3. (continued)

	Married over entire time[a,b]			Recently widowed[a,b]			Widowed over entire time[a]		
	Time 1	4 yrs. later	Diff.	Married time 1	Widowed 4 yrs. later	Diff.	Time 1	4 yrs. later	Diff.
IV. Financial situation (1950s)									
Gotten better in last few years	33%	23%	−10	6%	0%	−6	19%	13%	−6
Gotten worse	17	18	− 1	37	44	−7	36	29	+7
Satisfaction with present financial situation									
Pretty well satisfied	51	47	−4	31	38	+7	43	48	+5
Not satisfied at all	9	14	−5	6	25	−19	16	23	−7

a. In the 1970s panel, the Ns are Married over entire time—386; Recently widowed—16; Widowed over entire time—95. In the 1950s panel, the Ns are Married over entire time—418; Recently widowed—10; Widowed over entire time—59.

b. Percentages shown for those "married over entire time" and "recently widowed" are standardized in terms of the age distribution of those "widowed over entire time."

insurance benefits may seem a boon until the realization sets in that they are inadequate. Instead of short-term traumatic effects, the final wave for such reasons might reveal improved morale that would decline with the prolongation of widowhood. The more we ponder the case of the recently widowed, the shakier become our preconceptions. Openmindedness is in order in approaching the data.

On the first item in table 3.3, overall satisfaction with life, the data come close to fitting the "obvious" model. The recently widowed report almost as much satisfaction on the first wave (when they are still married) as the persistently married and considerably more than the persistently widowed. Considering their problems in the last stages of their marriage, the finding is anything but obvious. The tone of their feelings is surprisingly temperate. Four years later, shortly after widowhood, there is a sharp decline in their satisfaction, and the level then is about the same as among the persistently widowed. Here, too, the findings are far from obvious. The recently widowed, like the persistently widowed, rarely report extreme dissatisfaction, and the great majority describe their lives as "pretty satisfying." The earlier dramatic finding among the persistently widowed cannot be explained away by the theory that extreme dissatisfaction is dissipated with time.

The next four items are drawn from the fatalism battery within the larger scale on personal competence. As the reader will recall, a large number of tests had yielded considerable evidence of greater fatalism among the persistently widowed, of a sense that life was beyond their personal competence to control. Among the recently widowed, the evidence is mixed, and the fewer tests available unfortunately make it difficult to draw firm conclusions. One thing is clear. The recently widowed showed a much more radical change in the direction of fatalism in the four-year interval between their marriage and widowhood than either the persistently widowed or married over the same period. (On one item out of the four they did not change but the persistently widowed also showed no change, suggesting that it may be less sensitive than the other questions in the battery.) On two of the other items, initially the recently widowed are even less fatalistic than the married, but by the final wave four years later, they have moved toward or a bit beyond the persistently widowed in fatalism. The pattern on these items fits the "obvious" model, although there is no indication of temporary, massive effects that are washed away with time. However, on the first item shown the recently widowed report an extremely high level of fatalism initially, perhaps in response to the afflictions that struck many in the last stage of their marriages. The level becomes more extreme—almost universal among them—four years later. The pattern on this one item fits the model of temporary, massive effects that weaken with time.

On the two contrasted items from the political efficacy scale, the tests are replicated from the 1950s and 1970s panels. On the item where personal competence is seen as the source of efficacy, the recently widowed show a small, almost negligible decline in self-regard shortly after widowhood whereas the persistently widowed show no changes with time. Despite the change, the final score reveals greater self-regard among the recently widowed. Here again there is no evidence of a temporary massive effect that is attenuated with the prolongation of widowhood. On the other efficacy item where the fault is put upon government officials for their lack of concern, again one observes the secular trend toward increasing cynicism between the 1950s and 1970s and continuing onward from 1972 to 1976, which the recently widowed shared with other groups. But in both panels the belief that government officials don't care about "people like them" is much less prevalent among the recently widowed than among the persistently widowed. The immediate aid and the benefits instituted shortly after widowhood may inhibit the belief until widowhood is prolonged and the widows realize that their persistent problems have not been remedied. The findings once again do not support a theory of temporary, massive effects that wear off with time.

On the three items drawn from the political cynicism scale shown next in the table, the recently widowed behave in strange and confusing ways that deter any simple and easy explanation. On the first item, the belief in the moral integrity of the government, the recently widowed reject the steep secular trend toward distrust of government, which defies understanding. However, the unusual pattern on the other two items coupled with the unusual pattern on the earlier question of whether government officials care about them does suggest a tentative conclusion. Shortly after widowhood their cynicism declined radically. They were far less likely to believe that government wastes tax money and is run for the benefit of big interests. One speculates that the immediate help provided may allay such beliefs, which emerge only with prolonged widowhood and persistent problems. Whatever the explanation, the findings on these two items again give no support to the theory of temporary, massive negative effects.

The combined evidence from the three misanthropy items shown next in the table is clearly weighted against the theory of temporary, massive negative effects. While in the last stage of their marriages the recently widowed display more bitterness about others than the married on the first two items, and as much or more bitterness than the persistently widowed. At that point, on the third item they display no more bitterness than the persistently married or widowed, but surely no less. Shortly after widowhood, indeed, they change a lot and much more than either the persistently married or widowed. However, the change on two of the three items is in a positive direction. Bitterness has become much less prevalent among the recently widowed.

In the area of social and spiritual involvement the recently widowed show a distinctive and generally consistent pattern. On the first wave of measurement prior to widowhood, they were less likely to attend religious services every week and to listen to the 1952 presidential campaign on the radio than either the persistently married or widowed. Also in 1952 they were less likely than the persistently married to watch the campaign on television or to read about it and they shared with the persistently widowed a relatively low level of such viewing and magazine reading. Our earlier suggestion about the drains on their time and energies from the afflictions that struck in the last stage of their marriages may be the explanation. The steep rise in their TV viewing after widowhood (steeper than the general trend toward television exhibited in the other groups) may also reflect the newly released time at their disposal.[36] On the last item the relatively high level of general interest in politics they report when still married is perhaps not consistent with their behavior as indicated by the other items. In any case, there is no evidence of decline in interest shortly after widowhood. The findings on all the measures of social involvement provide no support for the theory of temporary, massive effects among the recently widowed.

The reactions of the recently widowed to their financial situation in the 1950s, shown in the last set of items in the table, should be seen against the objective background. Although the question on income asked in 1956 was crude (asking for an estimate of what would be accrued by the end of the current year), the results do convey the circumstances of the recently widowed when they were in the last stage of their marriages.

Among the young, the 1956 median income of $4,999 of the recently widowed when they were in the last stage of their marriages was slightly lower than the $5,352 figure for the persistently married, but far higher than the $3,600 of those who were already widowed. Among the older, the $3,333 median income of the recently widowed at the point when still married, was considerably below the $4,440 figure of the persistently married, but nowhere as low as the $1,285 figure of those who were already widowed. The pattern in the 1970s panel reported earlier was the same, although income naturally had risen in all three groups in more recent times. As one can see, no matter what one's marital status, age brings poverty in its wake; so, too, does widowhood. But as the poet wrote, "Coming events cast their shadows before," and the incomes of those not yet, but soon to become widowed were already on the decline.

The first item shown in table 3.3 traces this process of decline. On the 1956 wave of the panel the recently widowed, then in the last stage of their marriages, were much more likely than the other two groups to reveal a net change for the worse. In the same period a third of the persistently married and a fifth of the persistently widowed reported their situation had improved in comparison with 6 percent among the recently widowed. Four years later, shortly after their widowhood, not one of the recently widowed reported any improvement in her situation. About a quarter of the persistently married, already relatively well off, fortunately became even better off over the same period, and a small but not trivial number of the persistently widowed, 13 percent had experienced an improvement. Close to half, 44 percent of the recently widowed reported that their situation had gotten worse in the first few years of their widowhood, whereas 29 percent, fewer though far from a trivial number of the persistently widowed reported a decline in the same period. This is one of the very few variables where there is clear evidence of a temporary massive effect that is attenuated, but not eliminated with the prolongation of widowhood.

The reaction of the recently widowed to their low incomes and to the worsening of that income and their overall financial situation, shown next in the table, is emphatic and negative. In 1956, when still married, they were much less likely than the persistently married to say that they were "pretty well satisfied" (the highest category in the three-point scale incorporated in the question). And they were somewhat less likely than those already widowed to report that high level of satisfaction. Four years later, shortly after their widowhood, the change in satisfaction is sharper than in the other two groups. One quarter of the recently widowed report that they were "not satisfied at all" with their present financial situation and less of them report high satisfaction than the other groups.

The area of finances provides one of the rare instances where there is a temporary, massive negative effect evidently in response to the rapid changes these women began to experience shortly before their actual widowhood. Yet even among the recently widowed the paradoxical pattern that characterized the persistently widowed is present in some degree. Despite the rapid descent, still no more than a quarter of them expressed extreme dissatisfaction, far less than the proportions who reported that they were "pretty well satisfied" or "more or less satisfied." The mystery of how and why the recently widowed as well as the persistently widowed have fortified their spirits against severe deprivation remains. Surely it is a testament to their strength but no warrant for their neglect.

The modest, far from massive effects among the recently widowed agree with the modest findings among the persistently widowed, but seem in disagreement with the studies in the literature, many of which dealt with recently widowed individuals. The methodological inadequacies of those studies and the specialized universes to which they refer as well as the narrow range of effects examined may account for much of the apparent disagreement. But the fact that many of those studies examined effects very shortly after widowhood, within the first three to twelve months in contrast with our longer interval may also explain the disagreement. Those effects might be labeled "immediate"; ours might be labeled "recent". Thus, though our study may not dispute such earlier findings, it may place them in their proper perspective.

Effects in the Late 1950s and Mid-1970s

Our longitudinal analysis of the effects of widowhood was based on two national panel studies, one conducted from 1956 to 1960 and the other from 1972 to 1976. Until now we have treated them as replications, simply as two independent series of nationwide tests of the same problem, each series adding weight to the body of evidence and strengthening the general conclusions. But this is to ignore the obvious difference between the two panels.

In the sixteen years that separated the panels the historical changes that occurred might have modified the effects of widowhood. By the mid-1970s, presumably, America had come closer to recognizing widowhood as a social problem and attempts to remedy earlier neglect had been set in motion. Self-help organizations have been formed; self-help manuals have been written; geriatric centers and other agencies have provided more services and supports for the bereaved. The problems of widowhood have been popularized by auto-biographical writings and the mass media. Perhaps the larger Woman's Move-ment has given support specifically to widows. Apart from whatever concrete help, great or little, has been provided, the recent developments might have changed the way widows define their situation. They may have read too much meaning into empty symbols, but nevertheless they might no longer see them-selves as alone, neglected by the larger society. Consequently the negative effects of widowhood might have been greater in the earlier period but gone unnoticed because we had ignored, except for an occasional glaring secular trend, the historical distinction between the two sets of data. If our vision was poor and our judgment tilted too far by the combined weight of the evidence from the SRC and the NORC surveys in the 1970s, the conclusion that the long-term effects of widowhood are few and modest in magnitude may be too global.

Re-examination of table 3.2, focusing only on the findings from the 1950s does not change the general conclusion. Only occasional and modest effects are ob-served. What had not been noticed before may be worth noting now. Although widows in both periods were more likely than the married to believe that government officials don't care about them, the difference between the two groups (not the level that was elevated in all groups by the secular trend) was greater in the 1950s. Ironically, some recent actions may have made the feelings of neglect less acute while other developments have not yet created a sense of grievance, and all the while the actual deprivation of widows has persisted. What shape these feelings have taken since the mid-1970s deserves an answer but is beyond the reach of our data.

4. Conclusion

Our study of the effects of widowhood is drawn from nine surveys of well-designed nationwide samples of the American adult population, conducted originally by two centers noted for the quality of their research. Its generalizability is not hampered by the small, sometimes biased samples of narrow, occasionally eccentric universes employed in earlier studies, and it does not suffer from many of the methodological deficiencies that characterized much of the research of the past. All of the analysis is based on a quasi-experimental design containing two control groups, married and divorced or separated women, who, when compared with the widowed, served to isolate the distinctive effects of irrevocable bereavement. In all these comparisons the controls over sex, age, and race reduced the ambiguity that otherwise would surround the conclusions, and the knowledge of many other features of the three groups, also incorporated in various ways in the analysis, further reduced the ambiguity. Vagueness, as well as ambiguity, was reduced by these procedures, and the conclusions became pointed concretely, though broadly, at the situation of white widows at two age levels across the nation.

The separate analyses of two sets of surveys, both nationwide but very different in design and conducted by different agencies, strengthened the overall conclusions, the weaknesses inherent in each set being offset by the strengths of the other set. The two SRC panels taken together examined effects in the 1950s as well as the 1970s via a sample of 178 white widows. Although conclusions are not narrowly confined in time, they are based on only 178 cases, not a negligible number but nevertheless a small sample. However, the seven NORC surveys taken together yield an additional large pool of 464 white widows although they span only the years 1972–78, not a negligible interval but nevertheless a limited historical period. In the SRC analysis, despite the refinement of the comparison groups, the impurities that remained might lead one to understate the effects of widowhood. However, the NORC surveys provided avenues to purify the comparison groups and to estimate the residual impurities, thus correcting that potential source of error in the conclusions.

The NORC surveys are cross-sectional in nature, measuring individuals at only one point in time, and therefore various effects of widowhood may have eluded the analysis. Many widows were caught in our survey only long after their bereavement when earlier transient effects might have been dissipated. Conceivably other widows might have been caught too soon, before very slow, long-term effects had taken shape. But certainly we were not left in the dark. The information on recency of widowhood inherited from these comprehensive surveys enabled us to appraise such possibilities and to make empirical tests of short-term effects. Nevertheless, cross-sectional surveys set inherent limits on the analysis of the process. However, the SRC panels provided longitudinal data that traced further changes over a four-year interval in a group already long-widowed and also measured a group of newly widowed both before and after bereavement.

The NORC surveys may seem to be limiting in another respect. The synchronous measurement of the variables in cross-sectional data frequently creates uncertainty in causal analysis, since the two variables involved may be of such a nature that either one, in theory, could have influenced the other and preceded it in time. Which is cause and which is effect then is hard to determine. Although a cautionary principle is appropriate in many instances, it is not universally applicable and it surely stretches the principle to apply it to our particular analysis. Some variables are clearly unambiguous in nature and widowhood would seem to be one. It is an event, seemingly an "Act of God," governed by what Sumner called the aleatory element—the roll of the dice. Is it credible that the unhappiness or dull life a woman was experiencing, the "effects" we examined, could have caused the natural death of her husband? If such events could be influenced by psychic means one would expect far less widows in the world, since many would have taken the magical preventive measure of adopting a cheery and optimistic outlook.

A critic of the cross-sectional analysis still might summon his expert witness, Freud, who reminded us long ago of "striking . . . cases where the person seems to be experiencing something passively, without exerting any influence of his own, and yet always meets with the same fate over and over again. One may recall, for example, the story of the woman who married three men in succession, each of whom fell ill after a short time and whom she had to nurse till their death" (1942: 22). The critic, to be fair, must add that Freud's case was not only striking but, by overwhelming statistical evidence, rare. That woman was widowed *three* times. She, herself, may have loaded the dice. Or perhaps some mysterious psychic element predetermined her fate. But she certainly typifies, at most, only a few cases in our sample. And it should be stressed that the cautionary principle, assuming it has applicability, leads one to discount positive findings, apparent effects of widowhood. In light of the principle our general conclusion that the effects of widowhood are few and modest in magnitude is not undermined. It becomes even more compelling. The matter, however, need not rest on argument and the evaluation of general principles and expert witnesses. The SRC analysis did not rely on synchronous measurement but on repeated measurements over time. For the variables treated as "effects," the initial scores provided a baseline to determine whether the later scores were changes following the onset or prolongation of widowhood, and thus genuine effects.

In these ways, and other ways reviewed earlier, the combined analyses of the nine surveys created a strong foundation for the conclusions. This is not to suggest that the present study, even in totality, has no limitations or weaknesses. However adequate the overall sample size for the major conclusions on lasting effects among white widows, it would have been even better to have a larger sample. Then, surely the conclusions about recent widows would have rested upon a firmer statistical base and been less tentative. With larger numbers, circumscribed effects in specific subgroups, for example widows in their forties, could have been examined more sharply and confidently. However broad the domain explored for possible effects, it would have been better yet to explore a more varied and broader realm. If the surveys had covered a wider span of time than the 1950s and 1970s and countries other than the United States, the conclusions, however much generality they have, would have been still more sweeping. Then effects under different historical and societal conditions could have been examined. And the conclusions thus far are limited to white widows. The problems of the black widow and the white widower have not been touched on and deserve attention. Studies of those groups require special care, but the prerequisite is more surveys and a much larger pool of cases, from which the subsamples can be extracted.

Clearly the limitations of the present study are not inherent and irremediable in the research design and strategy developed. Growth is inherent in secondary analysis. By fall 1980 an eighth General Social Survey had become available, adding another seventy-odd cases to the refined and purified group of 464 white widows we employed. Indeed these new cases enabled us to strengthen the base for one special analysis of the recently widowed, although it was too late for them to be incorporated anywhere else in the analysis. Additional nationwide, high quality, cross-sectional surveys from other times and countries that contain relevant material are available targets of opportunity. Long-term panels are a rarity, but those few could also be exploited for further longitudinal study of the effects of widowhood. And if the methodological lesson learned in the course of this study about the ambiguity and crudity in measuring "marital status" by a simple, single question on current status is heeded, future surveys will substitute for that almost universal procedure a short set of questions on marital history. That will enlarge the resources for good secondary analyses of the effects of widowhood. And if the substantive lesson learned about the heterogeneity of the category "not married" is heeded, analysts will stop the common, crude practice of treating the divorced and the widowed—and even those never married—as one group that is compared with the married. Automatically, evidence will accumulate in the literature on effects of such distinctive statuses.

The present analysis was undertaken to urge on others, by example, a strategy of secondary analysis. That outcome of the present study, if it comes to pass, is as important as its substantive findings. In the spirit of showing future prospects, one additional small-scale comparative analysis will be presented.

Effects among White Widowers

For all the reasons reviewed, the same research design was employed to study effects among widowers as had been used in studying widows. Two control groups, married men and divorced or separated men were compared with widowers to isolate the distinctive effects and all three groups were drawn from the pool available in the seven NORC surveys. The widowed and married groups were purified by eliminating all those whose histories included a divorce or separation. By confining the analysis to white men, age sixty to seventy-nine sex, age, and race were automatically controlled in all the comparisons. Thus the risk of spurious conclusions was reduced but the findings, though generalizable to the nation, are limited to the "old." Widowers are so rare in the general population that the two SRC panels yielded too few of any age to undertake a longitudinal study. Young widowers are rarer yet, and even the pool of seven NORC surveys yielded too few age forty to fifty-nine to examine effects among them.

This design created, once again, an unambiguous and powerful test of the effects of widowhood, but it served an additional purpose. In establishing whether widowhood has uniform or differential effects among men and women comparability is essential, and it was achieved. Any differential effects to be reported cannot stem from the sampling method or the procedures and instruments used, and do not reflect differences in the age or racial composition of the groups of men and women. Other compositional factors that normally accompany and distinguish widowers and widows, of course, are still operative and may contribute to the findings, but this is intended and desirable in the inquiry. If it is in the nature of the situation that widowhood does not produce, for example, as much financial hardship for men as it does for women and this might mediate a differential effect, it should be included in the reckoning. Table 4.1 presents the profiles of the three groups of men as a context for interpreting the later findings on effects. Reference back to the relevant half of table 2.1 (the profiles of women) will reveal any nationwide differences in the composition of old white widows and widowers that might account for differential effects, and the most striking of these will be noted for the reader.

Old widowers, like widows, are much poorer than their married counterparts and the great majority of them live alone. However, in terms of absolute income widowers are not as poor as widows, which one would expect since the death of the wife probably would not produce as much loss of earnings as the death of the husband. Insofar as the children of older individuals still create financial burden, widowers have another advantage over widows. They have fewer children, although the difference between the two groups is small. Insofar as the children provide economic and psychic support, the widowers are a bit worse off. In other respects, as with the widows, widowers and their married counterparts have very similar profiles.

Divorced or separated men in the age cohort sampled are very few, and although the small sample makes the findings most tentative, the striking features deserve to be noted. The divorced or separated older men, like the widowers, are much poorer than their married counterparts, and are the poorest of the

Table 4.1. The profiles of widowed, married, and divorced or separated white men (Pooled data, NORC annual national surveys, 1972-78)

	Aged 60-79		
N^a =	Married 585	Widowed 90	Divorced or separated 46
Personal characteristics			
Total family income last year[b]			
Median	$8440	$6500	$4625
25th percentile	5125	4100	2160
Education attainment			
8th grade or less	38%	43%	57%
Grades 9-12	39	39	22
More than 12	23	18	21
Current religious affiliation			
Protestant	70%	64%	62%
Catholic	23	30	29
Jewish	3	1	0
None	5	3	9
Number of children (living or dead)			
None	15%	26%	22%
One	16	19	18
Two	26	20	24
Three or more	43	36	36
Current milieu			
Household size			
One person	c	74%	89%
Two	80	17	4
Three or more	20	9	7
Composition			
Zero members under 6	99%	100%	98%
Zero members 6-12	99	98	96
Zero members 13-17	95	98	98
Region living in currently			
South	31%	21%	27%
West	11	10	24
North	58	69	49
Size of place living in currently			
Large city	13%	20%	20%
Open country	21	14	26
Childhood milieu			
Father's occupation during childhood			
Median prestige score	43	40	41
Farmer or farm laborer	39%	30%	37%
Father's education[e]			
Eighth grade or less	72%	75%	83%
Grades 9-12	16	17	13
More than 12	12	8	4

Table 4.1. (Continued)

		Aged 60–79		
	N^a =	Married 585	Widowed 90	Divorced or separated 46
Mother's education[e]				
Eighth grade or less		74%	73%	82%
Grades 9–12		21	25	18
More than 12		5	2	0
Number of siblings[f] **(living or dead)**				
None		5%	4%	2%
One		8	6	4
Two to five		44	56	39
Six or more		43	34	54
Family composition at age 16				
Not living with own father and mother		17%	17%	26%
Reason				
Death of parent		81%	53%	92%
Divorced or separated		13	13	8
Other		6	34	0
		100%	100%	100%
Region living in at age 16				
South		28%	20%	30%
West		4	2	9
North		62	70	57
Foreign country		6	8	4
Native birth[g]		91%	89%	85%
Religion raised in[h]				
Protestant		71%	61%	66%
Catholic		23	34	34
Jewish		3	1	0
None		3	3	0

a. Depending on the characteristic, the bases used for the computation of percentages vary slightly from the Ns shown because respondents occasionally gave no answer to one or another question. Whenever the numbers that had to be excluded were of more than trivial magnitude, it will be noted.

b. About 6 percent of the respondents refused to report income and the bases are correspondingly reduced.

c. Less than one percent.

d. The Hodge-Siegel-Rossi scale was used to score the prestige of the specific occupations reported.

e. In about one-third of the cases the parent's education could not be ascertained for various reasons (fading of memory after so many years, etc.). The bases for the percentages shown are correspondingly reduced.

f. The question was worded in a fashion that included step-sibs and adoptive sibs in the count.

g. The question was asked in only two of the annual surveys, and the bases correspondingly are reduced by about 70 percent.

h. The question was not included in the 1972 survey. The bases correspondingly are reduced by about 14 percent.

three groups. Why this is the case can only be conjectured but one correlative fact should be noted. Their social origins, judging by their educational attainment and that of their parents were lower and their earning power, consequently, may have been impaired. (By contrast, although divorced or separated women were much poorer than their married counterparts, they were neither more disadvantaged nor of lower social standing than widows.) Most of the divorced or separated men live alone. Indeed they are much more likely to live alone than the widowers. The extremity of physical isolation they exhibit was not characteristic of women who were divorced or separated. It is pure conjecture, but it might be ventured that a divorce or separation among men in this old age-cohort would be likely to alienate them from their children thus leaving them more alone than women or younger men for whom either widowhood or divorce would not have the same consequence.

One last feature should be noted. From the question asked only in the 1978 and 1980 surveys, we find that 62 percent of the old widowers have been widowed for five years or less. Among old widows, by contrast, 64 percent had been widowed more than five years ago. However, since recency of widowhood (examined in table 2.6) had no influence on the effects observed, we may discount it in interpreting any differential effects of bereavement for men and women. We turn now to the findings on the effects of widowerhood presented in table 4.2.

Feeling Tone

The findings in this area among widowers show a basic uniformity with the earlier findings. Just as with widows, widowers have a less happy and exciting life than their married counterparts. They also report less satisfaction specifically with family life, but these negative feelings have not diffused into the other two specific spheres: satisfaction with the place in which they live and the satisfaction derived from friendships. Yet there is a subtle difference between the two sets of findings. Although extreme dissatisfaction has not become rampant, negative effects are more prevalent among widowers than among widows. One sees this most clearly in connection with family life, where 68 percent of the widows reported a great deal of satisfaction in contrast with 39 percent of the widowers. Let us reserve comments on this differential pattern for the moment. The findings among the divorced or separated men run parallel. They share the negative feelings of the widowers just as divorced women shared the negative feelings of widows. But the differential pattern is so emphatic that it almost shrieks for attention. On all five items, negative effects are much more prevalent among them than among divorced or separated older women. One sees this most dramatically in the realm of friendship, where 71 percent of the divorced or separated women had reported a great deal of satisfaction in contrast with 38 percent of the men.[1]

Table 4.2. The effects of widowhood revealed by comparisons of widowed, married, and divorced or separated white men (Pooled data, NORC annual national surveys, 1972–78)

	Aged 60–79		
N =	Married 585	Widowed 90	Divorced or separated 46
I. Feeling tone			
Overall happiness (self-rating)			
Very happy	46%	17%**	18%***
Pretty happy	45	53	56
Not too happy	9	30	27
Find life generally[a]			
Exciting	45%	26%***	33%***
Pretty routine	51	53	48
Dull	4	21	19
Satisfaction with family life			
Great deal or very great deal	84%	39%***	26%***
Some—quite a bit	15	44	34
Little or none	1	17	40
Satisfaction with place living in			
Great deal or very great deal	65%	59%	40%***
Some—quite a bit	32	35	52
Little or none	3	6	8
Satisfaction with friendship[b]			
Great deal or very great deal	71%	65%	38%***
Some—quite a bit	27	29	49
Little or none	2	6	13
II. Outlook			
Misanthropy scale[c]			
Most people can be trusted	51%	52%	47%
People try to be helpful	54	46	31*
Most people take advantage	27	26	34
Anomia scale			
Hardly fair to bring child into world[a]	39%	51%	64%*
Can't help wondering whether anything is worthwhile[d]	33	49[e]	55[e]
Have to live for today and let tomorrow take care of itself[d]	46	43	57
The lot of the average man is getting worse[a]	56	55	74[e]
No right and wrong ways to make money[d]	23	27	50**
III. Social involvement			
Spend social evening with relatives[a]			
Once a week or more often	35%	34%	33%
Several times a year or less often	33	34	29
Spend social evening with neighbors[a]			
Once a week or more often	23%	30%	42%
Several times a year or less often	52	62	46
Spend social evening with friends[a]			
Once a week or more often	11%	24%	29%***
Several times a year or less often	54	50	50

Table 4.2. (Continued)

	N =	Aged 60-79		
		Married 585	Widowed 90	Divorced or separated 46
Go to a bar or tavern[a]				
Once a week or more often		8%	9%	33%***
Several times a year or less often		83	81	46
Number of voluntary association memberships[a]				
Zero		24%	32%	48%*
One		28	30	20
Two or more		48	38	32
Attend religious services				
Never		13%	16%	36%***
Several times a year or less		32	37	29
Once or twice a month		14	17	20
Nearly every week or every week		34	21	13
More than once a week		7	9	2
Hours of television viewing per day				
Zero		1%	3%	21%***
Four or more		30	41	26
Median		2.5	2.8	1.8
Read the newspaper[a]				
Daily		84%	79%	70%**
Never		3	2	17
IV. Financial situation				
Getting better last few years		27%	25%	18%
Getting worse		22	22	30
Not at all satisfied with present situation		15%	17%	40%***
V. Health				
General health (self-rating)[f]				
Excellent or good		60%	47%[e]	49%
Fair or poor		40	53	51
Satisfaction with health[b]				
Great deal or very great deal		56%	41%**	45%**
Some—quite a bit		35	39	25
Little or none		9	20	30

*** Difference between married and widowed (or married and divorced) by two-tailed chi-square test significant at p ≤ 0.001.
** Significant at p ≤ 0.01 > 0.001.
* Significant at p ≤ 0.05 > 0.01.
a. Asked in only four of the seven annual surveys. The bases correspondingly are reduced by about 40 percent.
b. Asked in six of the seven annual surveys. A seven-point rating scale was shown the respondent with the three middle points labeled "some," "fair amount," "quite a bit."
c. Asked in five of the seven annual surveys.
d. Asked in only three of the seven annual surveys.
e. By a one-tail test the difference between married and widowed (or married and divorced) would be regarded as significant at the level p ≤ 0.05.
f. Asked in six of the seven annual surveys.

These findings should shatter any stereotype about the sporting life of older men who are alone. Instead it is a sad life, and seems to be especially so for those who are divorced or separated. The pattern is puzzling only when we focus exclusively on the economic sphere. To be sure, as documented, the widower's finances are less severe than the widow's, and he is less dependent on others for financial aid. He may still have his job to keep him busy. But consider other aspects of his life. As Berardo and others have speculated, he has lost the homemaker-housekeeper on whom he generally depended for his domestic wants. Often he cannot manage alone, whereas the widow is capable of managing domestic matters quite well despite the loss of the husband. And for various reasons, the widower is less likely to receive help from others. The formulation applies equally to older men who are divorced or separated. In a study of the aged widowed in Thurston County, Washington, Berardo obtained empirical evidence that agrees with our nationwide findings and supports these speculations. His aged widowers were the most isolated socially, least likely to be living with children and receiving various forms of assistance from them, and were the least satisfied with their close friendships (1970).[2]

Outlook on Life

The new findings in this area for old widowers and the earlier findings for old widows are uniform. As with widows, on almost every test misanthropy and anomia are equally prevalent among old married men and widowers. The negative feelings have not invaded the widower's philosophy of life. But the old divorced or separated men are consistently, generally significantly, and substantially more anomic than their married counterparts, which contrasts with the earlier pattern among older divorced or separated women who showed less marked, consistent effects. The old divorced or separated men are set apart from other groups—married or widowed, men or women—by their negative feelings and their negative outlook on life and society.

Social Involvement

Widowhood was found earlier to have no negative effects on informal social relations of older women. If anything, it heightened such social interaction. Among men, widowhood also has no negative effects, but on the other hand, there is no evidence of any significant heightening of such behavior. Among old, divorced or separated men and women the findings are uniform. Informal social relations outside of the family are heightened, but the effect is more marked among the men.

Among both the old widowers and widows, the findings on formal involvement through membership in voluntary associations are uniform. They do not differ from their married counterparts. Once again, a differential effect of divorce or separation can be observed among older men and women. Membership is significantly and substantially less common among the men than among their married counterparts. Among the women, although the difference between the divorced and the married is suggestive and in the same direction, it is not significant. This is the third clear demonstration of the marked negative effects of divorce or separation on older men.

Widowhood, whether among older men or women, has no effect on social (and/or spiritual) involvement as indicated by attendance at religious services.[3] However, divorce or separation does make a difference both among older men and older women. They attend rarely or never in contrast with their married or widowed counterparts.

On the last indicators of social involvement, the use of the media, the new findings among old widowers and the previous findings for old widows uniformly show that widowhood has, at worst, trivial effects in depressing such involvement. But we find a striking differential pattern among divorced or separated men. Their involvement in the wider world via the media is much less than that of married or widowed men. Among the older women, the divorced or separated differed from their counterparts but not as sharply or consistently. Again, the evidence emphasizes the wide, negative effects of divorce or separation among men.

Financial Situation

Old widowers, like old widows, do not differ from their married counterparts in their satisfaction with their financial situation. Despite their relative deprivation, the response is mild. Very few of them—whether men or women—express extreme dissatisfaction, most of them accepting their privation or perhaps resigned to it. Dissatisfaction was more prevalent among older women who were divorced or separated than among their married or widowed counterparts. However, the difference was not great, and the response, considering their deprivation, could also be described as temperate or mild. In older men again there is a distinctive, differential effect of divorce or separation. Extreme dissatisfaction is so widespread that it almost reaches majority proportions. One cannot help but be struck by the general theme of a sweeping, negative effect.

Health

Among older women, the three groups did not differ in their satisfaction with health. The response certainly was mild considering the fact that the divorced or separated group had a history of much more frequent disability or hospitalization. Older men show a differential pattern. Both the widowed and the divorced or separated are more likely to report poor health than the married, and correspondingly they express less satisfaction.[4] However, once again, the divorced or separated distinguish themselves sharply. Extreme dissatisfaction is much more common among them and reaches substantial proportions.

That old widowers show more negative effects than old widows becomes a compelling finding when the risks of "survivor bias" are taken into account.

Recall the facts previously presented. Old widowers suffer higher mortality than their married counterparts, but widows do not. Widowers remarry more frequently than widows. Thus, the relatively gloomy findings for widowers were obtained on a sample that excluded the moribund and those who presumably found living alone intolerable. If it had been possible to include the not insignificant number who had died or remarried, the findings would have been even gloomier.[5] But since death and remarriage are much rarer among widows, the rosy tint of those findings would hardly have darkened with the inclusion of the widows who were lost from our sample.

Afterthoughts

Our small scale study of widowers accidentally revealed the sweeping negative effects on older men of bereavement following divorce or separation.[6] That the bereavement of widowhood is traumatic but less so than divorce is an ironic and paradoxical finding. To be sure, we must regard the findings as tentative, considering the very small sample of divorced or separated men in this age cohort. Yet the evidence is so consistent and dramatic that it cannot be ignored. Indeed serendipity, in the modern sense of the term, seems to have come our way via the avenue of secondary analysis. This anomalous and unexpected finding may lead us all toward new and promising theorizing about various forms of bereavement and then to new research, by secondary as well as primary analysis, that may be rewarding. Of course, unlike the Three Princes of Serendip in the fairy tale, good fortune is not the fate of the older divorced or separated men. They especially—and all the other groups of bereaved men and women—have had to bear the brunt of bad fortune. That so many somehow have learned with time to carry their burdens so well is to receive a message of consolation and hope from this study. That their burdens are heavy and their grievances growing is also the message of this study, and should not be ignored, Nor can we ignore the minority, few as they may be, who, throughout our findings, appear not to have learned with time to carry the burdens of widowhood well. For them, help must be a continuing obligation.

Of Time and Widowhood describes enduring effects, not effects that occur in the immediate aftermath of bereavement. That many may need help for a brief period is in no way denied by our study. That such help need not long continue, however, is documented by our study, which means that there is no excuse for not providing it.

Notes

1. Old and New Avenues to Knowledge of the Effects of Widowhood

1. For other studies flawed by the same basic sampling design, see for example, Anderson, 1949; Wretmark, 1959. Other early studies by Parkes (1964, 1970) were not confined to clinic patients and are not vulnerable to the sampling biases already discussed, although they raise other methodological issues that deserve attention. It should be stressed that Parkes was most ingenious in evaluating the various sampling biases in his studies of the clinic patients. He compared a matched subsample of the bereaved patients with the unbiased sample Marris (1958) drew from London death records, and he compared the findings for the twenty-one patients referred to him with findings from case records of ninety-four bereaved patients (of various types) who had not been referred to him. Of course, none of these ingenious adjuncts to a study would have been required if it had started from a less biased sampling design.

2. Clearly, the findings from the ninety-four cases examined simply via hospital records were not based on the one interviewer, but the original interviewers no doubt were not blinded to the fact of the widowhood and the illness when they asked their questions.

3. Glick, Weiss, and Parkes did extend the time span of their study by repeated interviews, phased from three weeks after the bereavement to a maximum of four years later. However, none of these studies expanded along the other dimensions indicated, remaining small in size, geographically concentrated, and restricted to a fairly homogeneous population of the widowed.

4. How much virtuosity is required is illustrated by Glick, Weiss, and Parkes (1974) who compared the demographic characteristics (available in the records) and causes of death of those in the final sample with those who dropped out, and who determined the reasons for the earlier refusal and learned of the subsequent experiences of those left out by a telephone interview two years later. How murky the nature of the bias is suggested by Danto's study. The introductory letter describing the inquiry to the potential respondents indicated "the fact that I was the Director of the Suicide Prevention and Drug Information Center. For reasons that may reflect much unconscious unrest within the widow group, these women were reluctant to cooperate, as they feared the main thrust of interest was in the area of suicidology rather than widowhood" (1975: 154). A fairer statement would be that the respondents thought that the inquiry dealt with widowhood and suicide and drugs, and perhaps had fears about the conjunction of the three. But no matter what the exact constellation of ideas, the implications for sampling and response bias must surely be considered, and defy any facile interpretation.

5. These investigators also showed their ingenuity by comparing the subsample drawn from obituaries with the subsample drawn from the unbiased frame of death records. Thus they established that, in fact, in many respects there were no biases and they were free to pool the two subsamples and build up the final number for their analysis to 109.

6. For a description of the control group and findings on morbidity in the two groups, see Parkes (1972: 201−4). Another most interesting example of this class of studies that employed a control group and involved a comparative study of American and Australian widows, both drawn from death records, is by Maddison and Viola (1968). The country differences suggest that social services in the area (in this case, the Australian National Health Service) have to be taken into account in any generalizations. In this study, admirable for its comparative and control-group design, the initial sample drawn from death records, as in the other studies cited, shrank severely and to almost the same degree in both countries: a 52 percent shrinkage in the Boston sample and 49 percent in the Sydney sample.

7. These investigators found substantial differences between the life satisfaction of recently widowed (less than five years) and long widowed individuals even when other factors were controlled, again suggesting that studies of effects among homogeneous samples of widows cannot safely be generalized. The generalizability of conclusions from localized studies also might be dependent on a subtle "contextual effect" that is often ignored. The proportion of old people (correspondingly widowed people) is higher in some areas of the country (e.g., Florida) and in communities of particular size (small towns vs. rural areas vs. big cities). Thus the widowed respondents might have fewer or more other widowed people surrounding them giving them a sense of lesser or greater support or common fate, depending on the area covered by the survey, and the effects might be intensified or attenuated.

8. See, for example, Hyman, et al. (1954: ch. 3). The questionnaire used in Lopata's survey was titled "Widowhood Interview" and the first two questions asked were: "How long have you been widowed?" and "What did your husband die of?" (1971: 208). This illustrates the way the instruments and procedures of such inquiries make the role of "widow" salient to both the interviewer and respondent.

9. For another illustration of this class of designs, see a study by Kivett (1978). She extracted the 116 widows contained within a larger sample survey of 418 old people living within one rural county that had included a question on loneliness, and then analyzed the factors involved.

10. Some readers may find this fourth class of studies anomalous and confusing to title. The analysis is done by the original, primary investigator, but not to satisfy the immediate purpose of the survey, although it is very closely related to that original purpose. To distinguish this mixed or hybrid class, the term I have used elsewhere, semi-secondary analyses, might be applied. For other hybrids within the category, see Hyman (1972: ch. 2).

11. Harvey and Bahr supplemented their nationwide findings on misanthropy with data on two other variables from two localized surveys, one conducted in four Illinois communities and the other from a highly specialized population in four California counties. Although this is the only example of secondary analysis of national sample survey data we have found, the analysis of available census data and vital statistics has been used as a source of evidence on certain effects of widowhood. See, for example, Chevan and Korson (1972) on living arrangements; Kraus and Lilienfeld (1959) on mortality among the young widowed.

12. The crude death rates over the entire twelve-year period for white widowers and married men show seventeen more deaths per 1000 man-years among the widowers, that excess being located in the group aged fifty-five to seventy-four. The maximum bias from mortality, although significant, is small in magnitude (Helsing, et al., 1981: 805). Attrition as a result of remarriage, however, also must be considered and its contribution to the overall magnitude and direction of "survivor bias" evaluated. While some take the morbid route that leads to the hospital or the grave, other might escape an intolerable widowhood by remarrying, leaving a rosy tint in the results obtained from the remaining group of widowed and adding a darker tone to findings on the married whose ranks have been swelled by those formerly widowed. Any reckoning of the biases, however, must include consideration of a compensating process occurring among the married, some of whom escape their intolerable situation by divorce, thereby eliminating those traumatized individuals from the surviving group of married who can be surveyed. These and still other aspects of what turns out to be a most perplexing problem will be explored in a number of places in all the later chapters. Although the perplexity cannot be completely resolved, the additional evidence to be presented will strengthen our previous conclusions. The findings among widows are relatively free from "survivor bias," and the contrasted gloomy findings for widowers become more compelling.

2. Nationwide Cross-sectional Surveys

1. For a summary of the General Social Survey, appraisals of the quality of the data, and a discussion of the opportunities for researchers, see the symposium review by Converse, Cutler, Glenn, and Hyman (1978). No survey was conducted in 1979 because of limited funds, and the data from the 1980 survey became available too late to be incorporated throughout our major analysis. The 1980 data, however, were used in the special analysis of the recently widowed where it was critical to enlarge the numbers of that very small but strategic group and to improve several specific estimates critical to proper interpretation of the general findings.

2. For the design of the sample, see *General Social Surveys, 1972–1978* (National Opinion Research Center, 1978: 1, 171-75). This publication is available in many university libraries and can also be obtained from the Roper Public Opinion Research Center, Yale University.

3. Marital status was determined by the question: "Are you currently—married, widowed, divorced, separated, or have you never been married?". On the reliability of the measurement see note 38. It is relevant to the earlier point about control over bias provided by the double-blind feature of secondary analysis to note that the question on marital status was asked as late as no. 21 or later in three of the surveys and as early as no. 8 in only one of the seven annual surveys.

4. See note 37 for such results.

5. Lopata's remarks bring to mind still another anomalous type of widow: those who de facto are remarried but who have not legalized that union and label themselves "widows" because of the possible loss of some benefit reserved for widows. Conjectures abound about this ironic situation—widows who are forced to "live in sin" in order to reduce hardship. In the nature of the case, evidence on the actual

numbers is bound to be flimsy. It would be very difficult to screen and eliminate such individuals from the group of "widows" located initially in any inquiry—including ours. However, in our later analysis of widows who live alone, as revealed by the routine enumeration of the size of the household where such companions could be reported and counted without embarrassment or penalty (e.g., as roomers), this anomalous group has been effectively excluded in the appraisal of effects.

6. Maddison and Viola experienced the same dilemma in screening their sample of widows drawn from death records. "Twenty-five women were found ot have been separated from their husband prior to his death." It is clear from the next remark: "disregarding those who were . . . unsuitable" that they made the same decision as Glick, Weiss, and Parkes to exclude this anomalous group from the subsequent study of the effects of widowhood on morbidity (1968: 298). The ambiguity of the status "widow" is also suggested by one enigmatic finding obtained from a follow-up questionnaire sent shortly afterwards to women classified as "widows" in the March 1968 Current Population Survey. The study was conducted by the Census Bureau for the Veterans and Social Security Administration to provide more comprehensive information on the economic plight of young widows with dependents. In the course of her report, Mallan notes that "some returned the questionnaire, indicating that their marital status was other than widow though they had responded as widows in the CPS." These are referred to as "special nonwidows", and are described as "women who were known as widows but really were not" (1975: passim). Mallan never clarifies the mystery, but the ambiguity we have noted may well be the key in light of one finding. The special study, which excluded the anomalous group, found a lower percentage receiving social security benefits than did the regular CPS. Since divorced and separated women are normally not eligible for benefits, it seems plausible some of those known as widows were divorced or separated from the husband who died.

7. Impurities, of course, are buried in many of the studies of widowhood in the literature, but simply are not noticed by the investigator or brought to the attention of the reader. The magnitude of the impurities usually cannot be estimated from external sources since the studies often refer to specialized populations sampled in biased ways. Such impurities are buried even within that most authoritative source, the decennial U.S. Censuses. For example, in the 1980 self-administered census questionnaire (as in 1970), information on item #6, "marital status," is obtained by having the person mark one of five categories: "now married, widowed, divorced, separated, never married." No instruction whatsoever is provided for those in the anomalous position that they were divorced or separated when their spouse died and who must choose one label for themselves.

8. Women interviewers conducted 92 percent of all the interviews in the seven surveys. The effects of disparity in the sex of respondent and interviewer vary with the questions asked and are not necessarily large in magnitude. However, on balance, the evidence would suggest that our design reduces such sources of error. See, for example, Hyman, et al. (1954: 150‒67); Benney, et al. (1956: 143).

9. See, for example, "Final Marriage Statistics, 1974" (HEW, 1976). The study of mortality by Helsing, et al. (1981) discussed in chapter 1 also presents large-scale, long-term evidence on the remarriage of widows and widowers. Cumulative rates of remarriage computed out to six or more years after widowhood were close to zero for widows except for the very small group (about ten percent) who were under age forty-five. Widowers, however, have substantial rates of remarriage except among those over age sixty-five; the rates at earlier ages triple, or even quadruple the magnitude found among the widows. These two sources provide consistent evidence that any "survivor bias" resulting from remarriage which might distort the findings both for widows and married women, a potential problem raised in chapter 1, is very small in magnitude. Although it is tangential evidence, Marris reports that the rate of remarriage in the one year, 1951, for widows in England and Wales was only 1 percent for those age fifty to fifty-nine and 3 percent for all those age twenty to fifty-nine (1958: table 5, 60). The implications of the substantial rates of remarriage among widowers will be explored in chapter 4.

10. In the six surveys in the years 1972‒77, the proportion of black respondents interviewed by white interviewers was never lower than 22 percent, and was as high as 63 percent in one survey. See Schaeffer (1980: table 3). She also documents effects on the responses of blacks, especially on racial questions. For evidence of such effects in an earlier period, especially among southern respondents, see Hyman, et al. (1954: 159‒170). For evidence of such effects in surveys conducted by the Michigan Survey Research Center, the source for our data in chapter 3, see Schuman and Converse (1971). Given such sources of error, the reader may wonder why the safeguard is not routinely instituted. Black interviewers are assigned to neighborhoods that are known to be predominantly black. Consequently, no less than the minority of black respondents, those living in white neighborhoods, are likely to be interviewed by white interviewers.

11. Whatever small error there might be in generalizing about the total population from surveys restricted to English-speaking, noninstitutionalized adults is smaller yet in generalizing about white

women (widows and other groups) age forty to seventy-nine in the 1970s. Only the tiniest fraction of them would be serving in prisons or the army or enrolled in residential colleges. A very small fraction would be living in institutions or other kinds of "group quarters." For widows aged sixty-five to seventy-four of all races, the 1960 Census figure was 2.9 percent, and, of course, the figure would be much lower in the younger age groups in our sample. Those living in so-called "institutions" or "group quarters" because of bad health would be a still smaller fraction of all widows, once again documenting that the survivor bias resulting from morbidity is negligible. For a summary of such data, see Carter and Glick (1976: especially table 9.11, 284). Similarly, those who cannot speak English would be only a very small fraction of white adults age forty to seventy-nine in the 1970s—again clustered mainly among the oldest in our age range—and that fraction would probably be of the same magnitude among age-matched widowed and married. It might have been a larger fraction if blacks had been included in our analysis, a considerable portion of whom being Hispanic-speaking. Over and above the major analytical advantages already reviewed, confining this portion of our study to white women age forty to seventy-nine and examining effects separately for older and younger widows and their married counterparts thus makes the generalizations safer. Whatever cautions are necessary apply mainly to the specific data reported for the older widows and, as suggested in note 35 below, to the specific findings on their health. Although confining the major analyses to those under age eighty reduces the risk of biased conclusions, it does deprive us of knowledge about very old widows. However, a separate analysis of that important group, to be reported later, will remedy this deficiency.

12. Separate comparisons within the two age categories may seem too crude a control over age and inadequate to reveal a subtle differential pattern within a particular very narrow age group. As a check, a series of tests were rerun using four stages of age. The "young" were subdivided into those in their forties vs. fifties, and the "old" into those in their sixties vs. seventies. These results will be reported later along with the findings on the very old, those in their eighties.

13. To those readers unfamiliar with the circumstances of the widowed and who look back at these figures from the vantage point of the 1980s, the figures may seem so low that they may quickly conclude that the data are in error. Note, first, that the incomes are expressed in terms of the dollars of the 1970s, not adjusted for inflation. Other studies confirm the pattern. Mallan's analysis of the data collected in the Current Population Survey in early 1972 (based on a sample of 50,000 households) indicated that in 1971 the median income of all widows (black and white) of all ages under sixty was $4,140 for those with dependent children (entitled to special benefits) and $3,560 for those without dependent children. (Lucy B. Mallan, 1975). Our figure for the previous years' income, 1972–78, for white widows between ages forty and fifty-nine is $7,690, not so different when one takes into account the rising trend in earnings and the increases in social security benefits since 1971, and the fact that the most impoverished stratum, widows who are black, are excluded from our data. If we include black widows and all ages under sixty in our computation, and confine ourselves to the surveys in 1972 and 1973 (including 1973 to build up the base), thus increasing comparability with the CPS data, our estimate of the median income in the previous year, $6,636, is closer to the Census figure. Some of the discrepancy might also reflect the concealment of income from a governmental inquiry. In a second study of Chicago widows, Lopata remarks: "The refusal to disclose income is not surprising, since the study was sponsored by the Social Security Administration and all guarantees of confidentiality by the interviewers could not dispel the fear that information on income could result in the loss of benefits" Lopata (1979: 326). Some criticism might be leveled at a general measure of poverty based on cash income as a standard to appraise the poverty of widows. Specialized patterns of consumption and assets have to be considered. The General Social Survey did not include information on assets, but many other sources show the meager holdings of widows. For example, in Berardo's study of Thurston County, an index was computed from a battery of questions which provided information on inheritances, retirement benefits, savings, investments, and insurance as well as income. Seventy-six percent of the widows scored low on the composite index in contrast with 49 percent of the married. Berardo also reports that for 1962 "the Census data . . . indicate that widows have substantially lower assets than nonwidows in all age groups" (1967: 12). In a later paper, he cites a 1964 study showing the meager assets of widows (1968: 193). In Lopata's second survey of widows in metropolitan Chicago, a battery of detailed questions on the 1973 income of the widow and other family members from property rent, interest on savings, dividends from stocks and bonds, veteran's widow's pension, employee's pension, private insurance, and other sources was asked. From the nine sources together the median income was $6,714, suggesting that the assets were meager, and she reports that: "Only three in ten widows can draw upon 'interest on savings, dividends, stocks, bonds,' but the sums from this source are not large. 'Veterans widows' pensions' and 'employee pensions' . . . help only 10 percent of the women, while a widely held assumption that many widows benefit from 'private insurance' is dispelled by the fact that only two percent of the Chicago area respondents obtain monies from this source . . . (1979: 332). It should be noted that the sample was "representative only of women

who are current or former beneficiaries of social security as widows of entitled men and/or as mothers of that man's children" (1979: 57) in Chicago, rather than all widows, but surely the evidence shatters the vulgar image of the rich widow loaded with assets. The meager assets of widows is demonstrated even more dramatically by another study, albeit one focussing on a selected subgroup, age fifty-eight and fifty-nine contained within a large nationwide sampling conducted by the Social Security Administration in 1969. The median income received from assets in 1968 was $295 (mean was $679), suggesting how small average assets were. See Thompson (1980: 138–39). In the Helsing, et al. study of mortality, 18 percent of the widowed (men and women) were "living in domiciles with less than one full bathroom for . . . exclusive use," a vivid indicator of the quality of the homes the widowed own or rent and, more generally, of low socioeconomic status. The difference between widowed and married in the distributions of number of bathrooms was highly significant, the widowed having less such amenities (1981: 804 and table 1). Carp (1976: 254) summarizes other evidence on the poor housing and neighborhoods of widows. The well-traveled critic who met a rich widow resettled in Monte Carlo might argue that our surveys, and all the other surveys cited, exaggerate the financial plight of the widowed. Since the universe is limited to the United States or smaller areas within the country, those widows rich enough to settle into some lap of luxury abroad cannot be sampled, and their assets and incomes are not counted in any of these estimates. But the occasional rich widow resettled in Monte Carlo is offset by the poor widow who returned to her depressed village in Sicily in order to survive. And since the married as well as the widowed might well become expatriates whether to live in luxury or to survive, the comparisons between groups would not be impaired by the restriction built into all surveys.

14. A few other methodological tests are implicit in the table. For example, married women, unless in the rarest of circumstances (e.g., no children or grown children and with husbands permanently institutionalized or on extended duty overseas for the military or business), would not be living alone, and our table mirrors this fact. One percent or less live alone, suggesting that both household size and being married are measured accurately. Since our table is confined to white women, ever married, between the ages of forty and seventy-nine, sampled between 1972–78, direct comparisons with aggregate Census data on the total population should not be used to appraise the net error arising from sampling and measurement. For other methodological tests of the quality of the sampling and reliability of measurement, see notes 37 and 38.

15. The small differences on many of these variables are nonsignificant.

16. See Mallan (1975: 7–9) for studies documenting the two processes: that widows had lower incomes than nonwidows before the husbands's death (even after proper adjustments for loss of earning during the terminal illness), and that income declined substantially after his death. For another study documenting the greater risk of death among white males with very low incomes, see Evelyn Kitagawa and Philip Hauser (1973: 18–19). See also "Preliminary Findings from the 1978 Survey of Survivor Families with Children" (Social Security Administration, 1980). In our sample, as suggestive evidence that low income is the long-term aftermath of widowhood, note that for 63 percent of our older widows and 46 percent of our younger widows, the spouse had been dead for at least six years. Only 10 percent and 15 percent of the older and younger widows respectively had lost their husbands within the last year. And stronger evidence that income declines after widowhood is provided by the panel data presented in chapter 3. Consistent with our finding of the small initial disadvantage of widows, Helsing, et al., (1981) report that their widowed population (men and women of all ages) had significantly fewer years of schooling than their married population. For national data on the educational disadvantage of widows, see Carter and Glick (1976: 287–90) who theorize that some of the difference may reflect the greater likelihood of remarriage among the educationally advantaged, thereby suggesting "survivor bias," but note that this was pure speculation. Using a retrospective question on income prior to the fatal illness or accident of the husband and a question on current income, Lopata documents a dramatic drop in income following widowhood among widows at every age level. For the aggregate sample of Chicago widows in her second survey, median income dropped more than 50 percent (1979: 328–37).

17. Our estimate of the proportion of white widows living alone (averaged over 1972–78) is considerably higher than that reported by Chevan and Korson in their analysis of the one-in-a-thousand sample from the 1960 Census, or the CPS estimate for March 1970. However, those earlier figures do not fully take into account the long-term secular trend among the widowed toward living alone, include the black widowed, who are far less likely to live alone, and also include in the base those living in institutions (or other group quarters), whereas our base is the noninstitutionalized. If the various estimates were adjusted to be more comparable, the discrepancy would be much smaller. Indeed the March 1974 CPS, conducted at a timepoint midway through our 1972–78 surveys, computed on the base of the noninstitutionalized, yields estimates closer to ours. See Chevan and Korson (1972: 45–52); Bureau of the Census, Current Population Reports (March 1970; March 1971; March 1974; October 1974).

18. As relevant background another question in the surveys established that in only 5 percent of all

households with two or more persons was there an individual who was not a relative of the respondent, and in only 1 percent of the households was there more than one unrelated individual.

19. The presence of young children is doubled-edged in its implications. There is dependence and economic burden, but there is the benefit of social security payments for widows with children under age eighteen denied to those with older children. However, Mallan's analysis (1975) suggests the benefit is too meager to lighten the burden very much.

20. Mallan reports for all women (white or black) of all ages with children under eighteen about a $500 advantage in 1971 median income for widows as compared with the divorced or separated, possibly reflecting the social security benefits, which, of course, would not apply to either of our groups because of the ages of their children (1975: 6 and table 3).

21. For the exact wording of the questions, the conventions governing their use, format, the full range of alternatives or answer boxes provided, and the sequence in which the questions were asked, the reader is referred to *General Social Surveys, 1972–1978, Cumulative Code Book* (1978). It also includes interviewing and coding instructions, and the full distributions of results on all questions for the aggregate national sample in each annual survey.

22. Two special NORC surveys, focused on problems of happiness and psychological well-being, included the self-rating on "overall happiness." In the pilot study conducted in 1962 by Bradburn and Caplovitz in four small Illinois communities, unhappiness also was reported much more frequently by widows than by married women. But divorced or separated women, although less likely to be happy than the married, were happier than the widowed, in contrast with our finding. Since age was not controlled, the findings remain ambiguous. However, Harvey and Bahr (1974) who re-analyzed these data and compared the married and widowed (men and women) but not the divorced, controlling both age and income found that the difference in happiness persisted. In Bradburn's second study conducted in twelve large cities, widows again were much more likely than the married to be unhappy, but unhappiness was equally prevalent among divorced and separated women, as in our study. However, these findings also suffer from ambiguity because age was not controlled in the comparisons (1965: 13; 1969: 148–49). Our findings are almost identical to those Glenn reported in an analysis of the 1972–74 GSS using our two age levels. Widowed and divorced or separated women were about equally and significantly less likely to report being "very happy" than their married counterparts (1975: 594–99, table 1). Significant but very modest effects of marital status on happiness were also documented in another analysis of the 1972–73 GSS. (Spreitzer and Snyder, 1974). An analysis by NORC suggests that the prevalence of happiness among the married may be artificially inflated by 4 percentage points because of carry-over effect from an earlier question on marital happiness asked only of those currently married. Thus the difference, modest at most as shown in the table, would be smaller yet if adjusted for the artifact. (National Opinion Research Center, 1978. GSS Technical Report No. 6, p. 27).

23. Cosneck reports that 10 percent fell into his "freed" category out of the 103 Jewish respondents over age sixty in the Southern city studied. No details on the sampling procedure are given.

24. Using a one-tail rather than a two-tail test, perhaps better suited to the directional nature of the hypothesis, the differences remain nonsignificant. It should be added that in the version of the instrument used in these surveys, each question was couched with two opposing alternatives (e.g., people try to be helpful vs. people look out for themselves, and a third, volunteered, qualified answer "depends" was allowed and coded. Thus any differences that existed would not be obscured by acquiescence response set or by arbitrarily forcing respondents into one of two extreme and categorical positions. Harvey and Bahr (1974) analyzed one question on misanthropy used in a 1960 national survey asking whether people care about others and also found no significant differences between widowed and married when age was controlled.

25. As the text indicates, the five anomia items were couched in the "agree-disagree" format of the original scale, a limitation we must accept in a secondary analysis and whose influence on our findings is hard to estimate. The surveys contained nine "anomia" items. The five used were chosen *blindly*, prior to inspecting the distributions by marital status. Two items that tapped misanthropy rather than anomia in terms of the distinction and argument advanced above were eliminated and two were dropped because they seemed to have little face validity for the construct "anomia".

26. Harvey's and Bahr's secondary analysis (1974) included a survey containing an anomia scale conducted in 1963 on a sample of members of Christian churches in four California counties. Although the sample is very special in character and the results too intricate to summarize, it should be noted that they did not find consistent differences between widowed and married, an occasional positive and significant difference being contingent mainly on income.

27. The two middle categories of the seven-point rating scale given the respondent are omitted from the table and only the five categories at the tail ends of the scale are shown in collapsed form to simplify

presentation of the data. The percentages reporting middle levels of involvement ("once" or "several times" a month) can be inferred by subtraction. The finding is not an artifact of the collapsing of categories and the choice of cutting points along the scale. The chi-square tests were computed on the complete distributions ranging from "almost every day" at one end down to "once a year" and then "never" at the other end. And inspection of the detailed distributions does not alter the conclusions.

28. Lopata, by retrospective and current questions in her large and well designed survey of widows in Chicago, also documented a decline in membership following widowhood, which characterized her older widows as well as the younger ones, and reports a fine analysis of the factors involved (1973: 245–50). Harvey and Bahr (1974) also document less membership among the widowed (men and women) in their secondary analysis of the Bradburn survey of four small Illinois communities, but data from another survey they examine are contradictory.

29. As the reader can see from the table, attendance "nearly every" or "every" week is the modal pattern among the married and the widowed at both age levels. The aggregate distributions for the total national sample in every one of the seven annual surveys show a high mode at "every week" and a very sharp drop off at "several times a week."

30. In the course of a unique, large-scale secondary analysis of communications behavior based on a series of national surveys, Wright compared the use of various mass media and the interpersonal communications of married and widowed (men and women), controlling age. His conclusion was: "There is no systematic way in which the communications behavior of widowed persons differs from that of married persons, nor are there differential changes between the two groups by aging, with the possible exceptions that married respondents are somewhat more likely to discuss politics regularly than are widows and widowers and to watch daily television *news* broadcasts." It is worth adding that on the last two variables the differences are small in magnitude, and that the generally negative findings included readership of news magazines and discussion of local community problems (Wright, 1975: 396–97. Italics supplied).

31. Using as a norm the aggregate finding from combining the total national samples in the four surveys containing this question, 33 percent of adults (every age, sex, race, and marital status) show a middle level of newspaper readership, the older white widows who manifest this level thus not being deviant. Wright (1975) also found no less daily reading of the paper among his widowed (male and female, black and white) than among the married, at both younger and older ages, thus strengthening our conclusion about the young, and casting into doubt our finding of a modest decline in involvement among the old.

32. The finding is not an artifact of collapsing the original four-point scale presented to the respondent and of ignoring the finer distinctions between good and excellent, fair and poor. The complete distributions on which the chi-square tests were computed show the very same pattern of findings. For the interested reader, we note that among the old, 15 percent of widows report "poor" health and 11 percent of married; among the young, the corresponding figures are 7 percent and 4 percent.

33. Early studies documenting increased morbidity especially among the younger, recently widowed, are critically reviewed for their methodological inadequacies by Clayton (1973). A careful summary of more recent evidence is presented in "Marriage Is Good for Health and Longevity, Studies Say" (*New York Times*, p. C-1, May 8, 1979) which documents, in contrast with the neglect in the earlier literature, the equally high morbidity of the divorced.

34. A case history reported in an early study illustrates the point. "Mrs. P is a sixty-year-old Hungarian-born widow. . . . Since her husband's death ten years ago, she has been working as a domestic, living in the home of her employer. Even with a small income, she is satisfied with her current standard of living. . . . Mrs. P regards her health as '*excellent,*' *although she has had four minor chronic illnesses* and would be rated as 'fair.' . . . Despite the ailments, she has no regular physician but attends a clinic, 'though it takes you longer to find out what's wrong.' She receives some medicine from her employer and usually lets her relatives worry about her health. . . . Mrs. P is very self-reliant . . . quite articulate: 'If she's in good health, a widow should work, same as I am.'" (Kutner, et al., 1960: 55, italics supplied). The writers label this series of histories "composites," but add that they are drawn from the actual survey data and their agency files. The same point was documented long ago by the large-scale evidence NORC collected in its 1957 nationwide survey of people age sixty-five or older. Eighty-six percent reported illnesses during the four weeks preceding the interview. "The average number of illnesses . . . was four per person." Nevertheless, "More than half the respondents said their health was good. . . . In keeping with the contrast between the reported high prevalence of illnesses and the optimistic self-evaluations of health . . . only 30 percent . . . had seen a doctor or talked to a doctor on the telephone. . . . Only five percent of those who had not seen a doctor mentioned lack of money as a reason" (Shanas, 1959: 6). See also Ferraro (1980).

35. As indicated, these surveys sample only the noninstitutionalized population. Thus, those adults who are so sick and/or so lacking in people to nurse them at home that they are in hospitals or nursing homes at the time of the inquiry are excluded. And those who are relatively so healthy that they are in the army or in prison or in residential colleges (no doubt a tiny number among white women age forty or older) are also excluded. It is difficult to evaluate exactly how biasing these exclusions are for our conclusions. Certainly confining our analysis to those age forty to seventy-nine reduces the risk of false cnclusions since permanent or prolonged institutionalization for reasons of infirmity and chronic bad health is most characteristic of the very old. The number eliminated from the sampling, at worst, is very small, less than 5 percent even for people in their seventies, under 3 percent among those in their sixties, and still less among those in their forties and fifties as documented by decennial censuses. And if such cases were equally common among the married, widowed, and divorced, conclusion about the effects of widowhood would have been the same even if the permanently institutionalized could have been sampled, although estimated morbidity in each group would have been higher. Needless to say those who were sick and previously hospitalized but then recovered and returned to their homes are included, in theory, in the samples. In fact, a great many were, as shown in the table by the substantial numbers of respondents in every group (from 35 percent to 72 percent) who reported being disabled or hospitalized at least once in the previous five years. But we still have to reckon with the risk of bias from those "currently" but temporarily hospitalized who would be missed, and from those "currently" sick at home who might be inclined not to speak to the interviewer. The risk from these losses is reduced to some extent by the unusually vigorous and healthy, so "on the go" and "out on the town" that they also might be missed by the survey. The net effect on the findings from these losses depends on the numbers involved and their allocation among the married and widowed. The possibility of some residual bias cannot be ignored. But it should not be exaggerated. And certainly the risk of bias from the loss of those with a short-term, but life-threatening illness seems negligible in light of evidence that widows and married women do not differ in mortality (Helsing, et al., 1981). And for those who question our finding of no difference in morbidity between old married and widowed, it should be noted that high morbidity of widows has been documented mainly for young, recently bereaved women and not for old, long-widowed women. For one additional caution, see note 37.

36. This is not to suggest that the widows (or the married) respond in an irrational way, utterly unrelated to their objective past experiences of hospitalization or disability. For example, the cross-tabulation of the two variables shows among widows with any such history that 20 percent express little or no satisfaction with health whereas among widows with no history only 2 percent express little or no satisfaction. But the mildness and incongruity in response is still highlighted. Four-fifths of the formerly hospitalized group do not express extreme dissatisfaction, and one-third express a great deal or very great deal of satisfaction.

37. All seven surveys used a stratified, multi-stage area probability sample of the English-speaking, noninstitutionalized population in the continental United States, eighteen years of age or over. Because of budgetary restrictions in the early years and much experience that it works satisfactorily, the 1972–74 surveys carried the probability feature down to the block or segment level at which point the interviewer, following a specified path at specified times of day, selected respondents within highly restrictive quotas specified by age, sex, and employment status. Beginning in 1975, additional funding permitted NORC to employ a complete probability design, and in 1977–78 all respondents were selected by a probabilistic device. In order to check on the possible bias of the earlier design and to calibrate the effect of the change in procedure, in the two transitional years, 1975–76, half the sample was obtained using the looser, modified probability design of the earlier years and the other half by the rigorous full-probability design of the later years. For full details, see the NORC Codebook, p. 1, 171–75. We have compared the findings from the two half-samples in 1975–76 on fourteen of our dependent variables, to test whether conclusions about the effects of widowhood are biased by the looser design implicating about half our cases. Seven were variables where we had documented significant effects of some magnitude. On all of these: rating of general happiness, whether life is exciting, satisfaction with family life, whether finances had worsened, satisfaction with finances, social relations with neighbors, and voluntary association membership, our findings and conclusions would have been the same if the full probability design had been used throughout the years. We also re-examined seven variables where we had reported no effects. On the five indicators of anomia and misanthropy, our conclusion that widowhood uniformly has no effects on outlook on life would have remained unchanged. On the two variables relating to health, the self-rating of overall health and satisfaction with health, the looser design on which we rely for about half our data may have led to slight underestimation of the negative effects of widowhood.

38. In conjunction with the annual social surveys of 1972, 1973, 1974, and 1978, NORC conducted methodological experiments involving a brief reinterview with random subsamples of respondents after

an interval of three to six weeks using an abbreviated version of the original instrument. Fortunately, many of the variables—surely the important ones—in our study were included in the experiment, and thus the stability and reliability of measurement can be assessed. For our crucial independent variables and intervening variables—marital status, age, and race; education, income, and children—more than 95 percent of the respondents were classified identically in both interviews. For seven other variables used in our study to describe features of the profiles of married, widowed, and divorced women, identical features of the profiles of married, widowed, and divorced women, identical classifications were also obtained in over 95 percent of the cases. For nine of our dependent variables or effects: attendance at religious services, recent financial situation worsening or bettering and satisfaction with financial situation, ratings of happiness and health, are people helpful and trustworthy, newspaper reading and television watching—the classifications, averaged over all nine, were identical in 85 percent of the cases. The two least stable items showed 75 percent agreement on re-interview and the two most stable over 95 percent agreement. Admittedly, these experimental results were based on collapsing the data by dichotomizing the variables, whereas our study employs the more refined levels of measurement available in the data, which may be subject to more unreliability. But, on the other hand, not all of the inconsistency of response revealed in the experiment should be treated as error, since some of it, indeed, can be true changes despite the short interval of time between interviews. In that light, the reliability is even greater than suggested by the experiment. See Smith and Stephenson, (1979: especially 73–75). The NORC finding of 98 percent identical responses on the variable *marital status* agrees exactly with Kendall's finding based on examining data a panel study of over 500 respondents in Baltimore re-interviewed after an interval of six months (1954: 160).

39. The same logic led us to re-examine the effects of widowhood using more refined controls on age. For the same set of selected variables used in the analyses that follow, comparisons between married and widowed white women were made separately for those in their forties, fifties, sixties, and seventies. The previous findings about the magnitude of general effects, or lack of effects, and about differential effects among young and old were confirmed in every test with two minor exceptions that characterized the very young widows—those in their forties. It should be stressed that the number of such very young widows in our pooled sample of seven surveys is very small, given the rarity of such occurrences, in contrast with the substantial number of widows in the other age cells used in this analysis. The findings, therefore, should not be given much weight. Surprisingly, widows in their forties are just as likely as their married counterparts to report satisfaction with family life, reversing the previous finding. Perhaps less surprising is the fact that on one indicator of outlook on life the very young widows are more embittered, being much less likely to agree that "most people can be trusted." This reverses the earlier finding of no difference between married and widowed in such outlook either among younger or older groups.

40. To simplify table 2.3 and those that follow, the middle levels of satisfaction on the five variables are not entered into the table, but can be inferred easily by subtracting the two extremes shown from 100 percent. We also re-examined four indicators of anomia and misanthropy where we had previously found no effects of widowhood. It is a plausible hypothesis that the outlook on life would be especially sour among poor widows, and sweetened among wealthy widows. Our former conclusion that outlook on life is not affected by widowhood is unchanged by this more refined analysis.

41. The reader will recall that the variable available to us was number of children, ever born whether living or dead. Given the advanced ages of some of our widows (and the married), it is a reasonable assumption that some of the children had passed middle age and might have died from the diseases of adult life. And some offspring might have died in childhood. These possibilities led us to our choice of cutting points on the variable. The group with few children might in fact have even fewer living children—perhaps none left alive. The group with "many" children, surely would have some children still alive. Thus the comparison is bound to be a meaningful test, even though the variable we inherit from NORC is not ideally suited to the analysis intended.

42. For a sensitive and vivid account of the way living alone creates particular forms of loneliness for certain types of widows, but not necessarily for all, see Lopata (1971: 68–71).

43. Incorporating the 1980 survey throughout our analysis would have resulted in considerable delay and extra expense, since it only became available after the bulk of the data processing and analysis had been completed. It did not seem warranted in light of the substantial evidence already amassed. However, it was possible to buttress the evidence on the one question of recency of widowhood quickly and economically, which was warranted in light of its importance and the need to strengthen the small base of one survey.

44. The cutting point, five years, used in this analysis to divide the group into "recently" vs. "long" widowed was dictated to some extent by the way the variable, duration of widowhood, was coded in the original surveys, and by the need to produce larger cells for the tests. Even though about 10 percent of

the "recent" group were widowed less than a year, some readers might still feel that the "recently" widowed includes many who have already had more than ample time to readjust. Fortunately, the literature suggests that is is a meaningful division that would not obscure the effects of recency. In the well-designed although geographically limited survey by Pihlblad and Adams (1972), those widowed five or more years showed higher satisfaction than the more recently widowed. In their well-designed but geographically limited survey, Kutner, et al. (1960: 64–65) even found that those widowed for as long as nine years showed lower morale than those widowed for ten years or more. In their large-scale, cross-national survey of the aged in Britain and Denmark, Shanas, et al. (1968: 272–73) report the incidental finding that loneliness occurred more frequently among women widowed within the last five years than in those who had been widowed for a longer period. (The relevant table omits data from the American survey.) And given the ages at which widowhood occurs and the subsequent longevity of widows, it is far from academic to examine the patterns among those widowed more than five years. They are the substantial majority. In the pooled 1978 and 1980 sample of white widows age forty to seventy-nine, 61 percent have been widowed for that long. Among widows, black and white age fourteen to seventy-five in 1975, the CPS reported an average duration of widowhood of 8.2 years ("Marriage, Divorce, Widowhood, and Remarriage by Family Characteristics, June 1975," 1977).

45. Among the widows shown in table 2.6, whether or not recently widowed, dissatisfaction with finances is more prevalent than among the widows—old and young—shown in table 2.2. The reader should not construe the two sets of findings to be contradictory. Table 2.6 describes the pattern in 1978–80, whereas table 2.2 describes the pattern for the earlier, longish period 1972–78. Such dissatisfaction has increased. One can document this more clearly. Among all young widows surveyed in 1978–80 (those widowed recently plus those long ago), 35 percent are "not at all" satisfied with finances. The corresponding figure in table 2.2 is 24 percent; among all old widows, the figure has risen from 15 percent to 23 percent. On the other variables shown in table 2.6, the changes from the earlier period shown in table 2.2 are negligible. Those other variables dealt with intrapersonal and interpersonal matters not likely to be sensitive to the external conditions of the period, whereas dissatisfaction with finances is, at least to some degree, responsive to the changing economic conditions widows must face. The combined sample of widows (young and old) in 1978 and 1980 had a median income of $5,750 in the previous year, a gain over the running average for all widows in the period 1972–78 of less than $1,000. No wonder dissatisfaction in this sphere has spread—not that it is yet widespread. Earlier, widows were found to be surprisingly acceptant of their circumstances. Although what has happened may be only a straw in the wind, when combined with evidence to be presented in chapter 3 it may prognosticate an emerging grievance among widows about conditions beyond their control, which they sense can and should be ameliorated by government. These data can also serve to strengthen the earlier conclusion that low income is mainly a consequence rather than an antecedent of widowhood. Among the old widows who had been widowed more than five years, median annual income was $4,857, whereas among those widowed five years or less the median was higher, $5999. (The figures refer to 1977 and 1979.) If the loss did not follow widowhood, the income of the two groups, equally old, would not be affected by the duration of their widowhood.

46. In the search for severe effects among the very old widows, we also examined a number of the indicators of an embittered outlook on life that one would expect to be affected at very advanced age. Surprisingly, the very old widows did not differ from the old widows in the frequency of their reports that "most people can be trusted" or that they "can't help wondering whether anything is worthwhile." The only dramatic difference between the two groups that turned up was in informal social relations, the very old widows spending social evenings with their relatives much less frequently. No doubt the pattern would be true of the very old who are still married, being an accompaniment of very advanced age rather than an effect specific to widowhood.

3. Nationwide Longitudinal Surveys

1. Details of the sampling as well as other procedures can be found in the codebooks for the two surveys, available from the Inter-University Consortium for Political Research, Ann Arbor, Michigan. See *The SRC American Panel Study: 1956, 1958, 1960* (1972); *The American National Election Series: 1972, 1974, and 1976* (1979: five volumes). The basic sampling design and some of its intricacies are also reported in publications of the program of research which included the two surveys. See for example, Campbell, et al., (1966: 80–81). To be precise, the target population was the adult citizenry, those enfranchised in the period from 1956 to 1976. Thus the 1970s study like the NORC surveys in the 1970s, defined "adult" to include anyone eighteen years of age or over. In the 1950s study, conducted prior to

the enfranchisement of eighteen-year olds, those under twenty-one were excluded. However, this change in no way affects the comparability of our three sets of data, since all our analyses were confined to those thirty-five years of age or over. It may be of interest to note that the seven NORC surveys in the 1970s (which because of the very large pooled sample size yield the most precise estimates) found not a single white widow under age twenty and less than one percent of the married and divorced to be under age twenty.

2. The implications of excluding from the universe those who cannot speak enough English to be interviewed were already reviewed in the notes for chapter 2, where it was suggested that this restriction would have very little effect on the generalizability of the findings and would bear mainly upon the very old. The restriction of the universe to the noninstitutionalized and the sample, perforce, to those well enough to be interviewed was also reviewed in chapter 2, where it was indicated that those losses warranted concern mainly in connection with findings on health. Since that area of effects is not included in the Michigan Surveys, it is of little concern here. The new and special sources of bias in panel studies are treated later.

3. The larger program of research containing each of the panels involved five surveys, a survey being conducted shortly before and after the presidential elections in 1956, 1960, 1972, and 1976. However, for many reasons to be reviewed, we made no distinction between those before and after surveys, treating each study as a panel with three waves at intervals of two years. Although Neal Cutler of the Andrus Gerontology Center has used the 1976 survey for an ingenious secondary analysis of "Subjective Age Identification Among Older Women," no one, to our knowledge, has exploited the two panels for either cross-sectional or longitudinal studies of widowhood. Cutler's incidental finding (1978) that widowhood had no effect on subjective identification with the "old" (thinking of oneself as old), whereas other factors did, is worth noting. It is consistent with our general findings that enduring negative effects of widowhood are few.

4. Although we used data from any wave of the two panels, the analysis was limited to changes over intervals of two and four years. The interval between the pre- and post-election surveys in any given year was very short and the spacing of the two interviews varied widely for respondents, from four months at a maximum down to a few weeks or, in rare instances, only a few days. Very few repeated measurements of relevant dependent variables were available on both a pre- and post-election survey. It is noteworthy that real change in marital status plus unreliability of measurement was negligible over such a short interval. For example, none of the married or widowed women reported a changed status between the pre- and post-election surveys in 1956. In 1960, none who had been married or widowed throughout the previous four years on all the successive waves of measurement through the pre-election survey reported any change in status on the post election survey. As we shall note shortly, even over a two year interval, very few women showed any change in marital status.

5. One should realize that on the first wave of interviewing, the SRC surveys had not yet become panels. At that point they were still equivalent in design and sample to the NORC surveys described in chapter 2. And the earlier treatment of "survivor bias" is relevant and reassuring—but only up to a point. Since our major longitudinal analysis of the "persistently" widowed, married and divorced is limited to those who entered the panel and were repeatedly interviewed over four years, additional sources of "survivor bias" other than those already treated in chapter 2 must be considered. First of all, any panel requires greater cooperation from respondents. If substantial numbers refused to continue to be interviewed on successive waves and if certain types of widows, e.g., those most traumatized, were more prone to refuse than other groups, those remaining in the panel would no longer be representative and the conclusions about subsequent effects would have to be qualified. The risk is increased when many repeated measurements spaced over a short period demand substantial cooperation, but should not be exaggerated with a few waves spaced out over a four-year interval. A recent analysis of refusals in the Census Bureau's Current Population Survey that involves a heavy dose of repeated interviewing—four waves a month apart, then a breather of eight months, and then four more waves at monthly intervals—provides compelling evidence. The overall refusal rate was very low, and dropping out on successive waves was not related to sex or age (DeMaio, 1980). It should be added that since sex and age are controlled in all our analyses, even if such differential losses occurred in our panels, they could not distort the comparative findings. In panel studies that focus explicitly on widowhood and trace its changing effects over time, refusals on later waves of interviewing might be biasing. In Glick, Weiss, and Parkes' study, on of the rare instances of such a panel design, about one-quarter of the widows interviewed on the first wave refused to be interviewed on a later wave, the major reason "being their unwillingness to review painful memories" (1974: 22). Clearly, this might eliminate from their panel those who were more traumatized and who knew from prior interview that the inquiry had reopened their wounds. Secondary analysis of the SRC panels, whose primary focus was on politics and which

never mentioned the problems of widowhood, creates no danger from such a special source of bias. And there is no reason to think that losses on later waves from being "not at home" after several call-backs would selectively eliminate a substantial number of widows of a special type. The general evidence of the very low rate of remarriage among widows, and the evidence in notes 4 and 6 suggest that such a special source of bias is a negligible risk. A four-year interval also raises the special risk of a bias in later waves from the death of panel members, or their institutionalization for reasons of senility or other incapacitating disorders. Of course, all the groups in our research design—the widowed, married, and the divorced—faced such risks from normal aging, and the risks tend to be equalized by the controls over sex, race, and age that were exercised. But the widows conceivably may have been at higher risk. Therefore, a special count was obtained from the SRC of the attrition after wave one resulting from the death or institutionalization of all the white widows who were forty or older at the time of the first interview, along with information on exact ages. (The analysis of the SRC survey, like the NORC analysis, was restricted to white widows forty or older.) Careful records have been made and kept by the SRC of the reasons all cases were lost from the 1970s panel, those facts obtainable in almost all instances by inquiries of neighbors or household members or by the field worker's investigation. In passing it should be noted that three widows had "moved, left no address" after the first wave and could not be traced, nor whether they remarried or simply remained "fugitive widows" could be determined. All three were in our "young" category—two in their fifties and one in her forties. At worst, any bias from the loss of those three would be small in magnitude and distort the findings only for young widows. (Occasional fugitives probably also disappeared from the nonwidowed groups and any resultant bias not unique to a special class of widows.) Only one white "young" widow, fifty-seven years old on the first wave had died or become institutionalized, her loss from the panel occurring between 1974−76 by which time she would have been at least fifty-nine, introducing a negligible bias, at worst, into the results for young widows. However, thirty-two "old" white widows, all sixty or older on wave one had died or become institutionalized between 1972−76, potentially creating a substantial risk of bias in the findings on later waves for old widows. If these thirty-two could have been interviewed and added onto the seventy who remained widowed throughout the four years and remained within our panel, the results might possibly have been different. The thirty-two might just have been those whose widowhood was so traumatic that it led prematurely to the institution or the grave. But note that the oldest case was eighty-eight in 1972. When she died or became infirm at some point between 1974 and 1976 she would have been at least ninety years old! It hardly seems fair to attribute her decline or demise to widowhood. Also, note that the median age of the thirty-two in 1972 was 76.5. Their average age by 1974 would have been 78.5 which interestingly enough surpassed the average life expectancy on that date for all white women. It seems reasonable to attribute the decline or demise to the common conditions of aging rather than the special circumstances of widowhood. Other facts strengthen this conclusion. Note that the median age of those old widows remaining in the panel was 70.5 in 1972. Only five of the seventy "old survivors" were eighty years of age or older, whereas eleven of the thirty-two lost from the panel were eighty years of age or older. The survivors were not unusually healthy; they were just relatively young. Our conclusion is further strengthened by the findings of Helsing et al. (1981) presented in chapter 1 that mortality rates cumulated over a twelve-year period, adjusted for age, are no higher for widows than for other women. The combined evidence suggests that "survivor bias" from all sources does not distort the panel findings on the effects of widowhood. Attrition eliminates the relatively old from all groups rather than a prematurely morbid subgroup. In evaluating the problem, we could not draw upon the reasons for losses in 1950's panel, since so much time had passed that the data were no longer available. However, Campbell, et al., remark that attrition from death, senility or institutionalization did not distort the social, economic, or political characteristics of the surviving members of that panel (1966: note 80). The magnitude and character of attrition from death and institutionalization in the comparison or control group of married white women in the 1970s panel was also tallied, but should not be treated as evidence since the crude data are most deceptive. If anything, the findings could serve as further but false support to our conclusion. The median age of the married (young and old) who suffered attrition on later waves was only sixty, in contrast with the median of seventy-six among those widows (young and old) who were lost. This may seem to suggest that marriage is more traumatic in leading to premature death and institutionalization. All that it signifies is that married women, whether remaining in or lost from the panel, are on the average younger than widows. And their different rates of mortality and institutionalization are ambiguous unless adjusted for age.

6. Since there was no detailed inquiry into the full sequence of marital statuses over the life history, rapid oscillation in marital status in the intervals between measurements which cannot be detected is, in theory, a possibility. For example, some of our persistently married might have been married in 1956, widowed in 1957 but remarried in 1958. Some of the persistently widowed might have been widowed in

1972, remarried in 1973, and rewidowed as of the measurement in 1974. However, such rapid oscillations seem most unlikely in light of general knowledge about the rarity of remarriage among widows. And the minuscule number in our panels who exhibited such oscillations even over a four-year interval, and who despite their strategic value to the study had to be eliminated from the final design, is compelling evidence. For example, the number who were married in 1956, widowed by 1958, and remarried by 1960 was one; the number who were widowed in 1956, remarried by 1958 and then rewidowed by 1960 was zero. And the datum just reported in note 4, no changes in marital status between the pre- and post-election waves in 1960, suggests that oscillations over short intervals are negligible. Although that datum also documents the high reliability of the measurement, the critical reader may still be concerned about errors in the measurement of marital status on any single wave of the panel. With respect to random error the evidence from the methodological experiments attached to the NORC surveys (see chapter 2, note 38) is comforting. There is no reason why the Survey Research Center's performance would not reveal the same very high reliability of measurement. And the empirical evidence presented later in table 3.1 on the reliability of SRC measurements of other factual characteristics, equally or more difficult to measure than marital status, is also reassuring. Other evidence is provided by the numbers in our panels who exhibit presumably impossible patterns over the waves. We found only two cases out of over 1,100 who were classified as "widowed" on an earlier wave and as "single" on a later wave. An occasional "merry widow" might well think of herself at a later date as a "swinging single" but if we regard this pattern as impossible and indicative of error, it is of infinitesimal magnitude. As for bias in measurement—a constant error in reporting one's true status on all three waves—factors that would lead to the inflation or deflation of the categories "married" and "widowed," would seem weak, although divorce might be less respectable to some than to others.

7. Survey Research Center's field staff, like the NORC staff, is predominantly women (about 90 percent of the interviewers used on all the waves of the two panels were women). Thus, here again, restricting our analysis to widows means that there are few disparities in the sex of the interviewer and respondent, a comforting fact in relation to possible interviewer-effect on the data.

8. This does not imply that such so-called "panel effects" create response errors of sufficient magnitude to be of much concern. Especially where the waves are few and spaced so widely apart, one would expect the repeated interviewing to have little effect. Indeed experimental evidence suggests that even as many as seven interviews repeated over as short an interval as seven months create little panel effect. For a summary of some of those findings, see Hyman, Wright, and Hopkins, (1962: 33–35).

9. Since divorce rates rose markedly between the 1950s and 1970s—approximately doubling—the number who had a previous history of divorce or separation contained within the groups in the 1950s panel would be about half that estimated for the 1970s. The panel findings on the frequency of the pattern, divorced or separated on one or both earlier waves, and married or widowed on the final wave, would also be relevant in evaluating the proportion in the two groups with a history of divorce or separation prior to the first wave. In 1976, on the final wave of the panel, among the married women (incidentally all of them white, forty-four or older by then) less than 1 percent were divorced or separated during the previous four years. Among the widows less than 5 percent were divorced or separated during the previous four years. The fact that the figure is higher among the widows than the married again suggests the ambiguity in people's definition of widowhood. The incidence of such occurrences over a four-year period, as expected, is much lower than the cumulative total of such occurences over the total life histories of the married and widowed, estimated by the NORC question.

10. The 6 percent of the divorced or separated who had answered "yes" do not, as noted earlier, necessarily exhibit the sequence: married-widowed-remarried-divorced or separated. The question simply asked, for a specified list of relatives including "husband," whether and when he had died, but not whether he had died while still married to and unseparated from the respondent. Thus, some who had the sequence: married-divorced or separated-death of "spouse" might have answered yes. Although they defined themselves as divorced or separated, other women whose divorced or separated spouse had died might have labeled themselves "widows."

11. In choosing a cutting point on age to divide the panel samples into "old" and "young" that would be both meaningful and comparable to that used in the analysis of the NORC surveys, we faced a dilemma. Those who were forty to fifty-nine at the time they were initially interviewed in 1972, in the first wave of that panel study, and thus equivalent at that point to the "young" in the NORC surveys (who were measured only once at the very time when they had reached or passed forty) had become forty-four or older by 1976, the final wave of that panel, and no longer equivalent in age. There is no perfect solution to the dilemma. Ours was to cut age at different points in the two panels, using age forty to fifty-nine on the initial wave for the 1970s panel and age thirty-five to fifty-four on the initial wave for the 1950s panel as the boundaries of the young. In a sense we have it both ways, at least one panel group

comparable to NORC in age whether caught in the initial or final interview. The findings on the young in the 1970s are thus exactly comparable to NORC when the measurement of a variable occurred on the first wave, and the 1950s findings comparable (apart from historical changes) when the measurement of a variable occurred on the third wave of that panel. In comparing the two panels with each other, the young on the first wave of the 1970s panel are equivalent to the young on the last wave of the 1950s panel. In tracing changes over time, we are always observing the process at a slightly later stage of aging in the 1970s panel. The reader should keep these facts and problems in mind in juxtaposing the three sets of findings. Similarly, in the Michigan panels the "old" are not confined to those under age eighty for a variety of reasons. Those age seventy-nine in the first wave would have been eighty-three by the final wave, and choosing a cutting point presented the same dilemma already reviewed in the instance of the young. In addition, our concern to enlarge the cells and to be able to generalize to the noninstitutionalized "very old" led us to include everyone, no matter how old they were on any wave. Although the finding previously reported in chapter 2 already suggested that effects among very old widowed were not different from those among the old widowed, extending the analysis to those over age eighty in the Michigan panel strengthens the evidence. In this analysis, as already indicated, the old are never younger than age fifty-five, no matter what wave of a panel is being reported.

12. Although repeated measurements of social, psychological, and political variables are central to panel surveys because of the interest in studying such patterns of change, factual or background characteristics are generally measured only once for various reasons: assumptions that the measurements are reliable and the characteristics stable, the need to use precious interviewing time and questionnaire space for covering the broad domain of interest to the investigators. Thus not many factual characteristics repeatedly measured by identical questions were available to us to examine the stability and reliability of the profiles, and we used only those few that were central to our study of widowhood. Fortunately, the characteristic that was crucial for our analysis of the panels, marital status and changes in it, was repeatedly measured.

13. These findings probably give a conservative picture of the financial effects of widowhood. Since the death of a spouse frequently occurs after a long (and expensive) terminal illness, some of the recently widowed group, although still married on the first wave, were already experiencing the "incipient" effects of widowhood that stem from the loss of earnings of a very sick spouse. if their incomes could have been measured while married but prior to that final illness a more dramatic decline following widowhood would have been documented. Another ambiguity affects the analysis because of the inability to establish exact date within the four-year period when members of the strategic group become widowed. All that can be determined from the three waves of the panel is marital status at the point of the interviews in 1972, 1974, and 1976. About 40 percent of the strategic group who were married at the initial point in 1972 had already become widowed by 1974. But among the remaining 60 percent still married in 1974, some might have become widowed in that short interval between January and fall 1976 when they were interviewed on the final wave of the panel, and their 1975 incomes were accrued while still married. The median income in 1975 of the entire group thus may understate the economic effects of widowhood. The error is surely small, since it is inconceivable that many individuals in the subgroup involved suddenly became widowed in the same short interval in 1976. It is certainly a more reasonable assumption that the dates of their widowhood were distributed fairly evenly throughout the two years fall 1974–76. Uncertainty also surrounds the exact date when the persistently widowed became widowed. All that we know is that they were widowed as of fall 1972, on the first wave of the panel, and remained widowed throughout the period. A small number of them might have become widowed between January and fall 1972, and their 1971 income would have accrued while they were still married, although it is treated by us as postwidowhood income. Thus the disadvantage in 1971 of the persistently widowed is probably understated by a small amount. In the NORC data, the same ambiguity is present, but the understatement is smaller, probably negligible in magnitude since field work for the surveys always occurs in early spring rather than fall.

14. The distribution of educationalattainment obtained from the repeated measurements on the 1956 and 1958 waves of that panel are almost identical in three of the groups. The only discrepancies of any magnitude occurred among the young widows, the group smallest in size where a change in a few cases can alter the distribution markedly. Net error of measurement (for error random in direction) is little, and less than shown in the table, since in fact a small number of adults (known from authoritative sources to be about 2 percent in this age band and period) return to school late in life and heighten their educational attainment.

15. Since we have shown only the distributions derived from the repeated measurements, only the net change is revealed. It is conceivable that the households of some widows shrunk in size and the households of others increased in size, these movements in opposite directions cancelling out each other

and revealing little or no net change in the total distributions. "Turnover" tables, a common procedure in panel analysis, would have revealed the changes that occurred among all the individual widows in both directions, but were not presented since our study is focussed on social-psychological effects of widowhood. The profiles of background characteristics are intended essentially as an interpretive context, for which the contrasted distributions seem sufficient. In the 1970s panel, although not in the 1950s panel, partial information on the specific composition of the household and the inclusion of some of the relatives was obtained in the 1972 and 1976 waves. By a special secondary analysis the nature of some of the changes that did occur among the younger widows could have been described. However, given the fragmentary character of the data, and the fact that the household arrangements of widows are only a background for our later findings and not a substantive focus, that analysis was not pursued. However, this note will alert other investigators to the potential of secondary analysis in illuminating this special problem, and the sources of such data are Variables #18 and #3020 in the panel.

16. Various methodologists have suggested recently that separating errors of measurement from true change in panel data can best be accomplished with three-wave data and have developed sophisticated models and intricate methods for treating this technical problem, giving added value to such data. See for example, three collected papers by Blalock, Heise, and Wiley and Wiley (1970: 101–17). Such a method was not applied, given its intricacy and controversy as to the best procedure.

17. For the classic paper on the use of this procedure in survey analysis, see Rosenberg, (1962: 53–61).

18. For the exact wording of all questions, the conventions governing their use, format and the full range of alternatives or answer boxes, and codes, the reader is referred to the codebooks for the two panel studies. These codebooks will reveal that occasional questions asked on several waves of the panel were used by us for only one point of measurement. On those omitted waves the question was asked of only a small subsample, making the datum too shaky to be included. A slightly variant form of the question on overall satisfaction with life, plus a battery of questions on satisfaction with specific areas, e.g., housing, neighborhood, etc. had been used in a 1971 nationwide SRC study of "The Quality of American Life." Widowed women, as in our comparisons, reported somewhat less overall satisfaction than married women with children over age seventeen (providing a loose control on age, but none on race) and divorced or separated women showed much less satisfaction. Parallel to our finding in chapter 2 that dissatisfaction does not diffuse into specific realms, the investigators report "There is a remarkable disparity between the way these widowed women describe their lives in terms of general well-being and the degree of satisfaction they express in the specific domains of their lives . . . they are *more* satisfied with their neighborhood, their city, and the country at large than is the general population" Campbell, Converse, and Rodgers, (1976: 398, Table 12.2 and 413–14, italics supplied).

19. SRC like NORC (see chapter 2, note 24) couched each question with two opposing alternatives, and a third volunteered alternative (don't know) was also allowed and coded. Thus, any differences in misanthropy that existed would not be obscured by acquiescence response-set or by arbitrarily forcing respondents into one of two extreme categorical positions.

20. For the secular trends on these and other items reported below, see Miller, Miller, and Schneider, (1980: especially 268, 278).

21. These three items were couched with explicit alternatives rather than an agree-disagree format, and were part of a larger set. Our three were chosen blindly, before looking at the tabulations by marital status, and the other items were rejected on what seemed to us ambiguities in formulation, or their loading on dimensions other than cynicism.

22. It should be noted that there was a minor change in the way answers "none of the time" were coded in the 1950s and 1970s panels, although the question itself asked of the respondent was identical in both inquiries. Inspection of the distributions for the entire national samples suggest to us that comparability across the two panels was not impaired. Of course, comparability in the way the answers of married vs. widowed were coded was assured within each inquiry.

23. A question asked in the 1958 wave of that panel may seem to be equivalent, but was not used by us since careful inspection of the content and the marginal distribution for the entire national samples suggests to us that the equivalence is highly doubtful.

24. Our twelve items were chosen "blindly" from a much larger pool of questions used on at least one wave of one of the panels. Items were eliminated for various technical reasons. Some had been asked of only a subsample and the statistical bases for the comparisons would be too shaky. Others had been couched in an agree-disagree format making them more susceptible to acquiescence response-set than an equivalent item couched with explicit alternatives which we chose. A few seemed to us ambiguous in nature. Our final twelve all couched with explicit alternatives provide an extensive battery, and there were practical limitations on the number of items we could analyze.

25. What is tabled on these four items is the percentage who answered in the extreme category, "disagree a great deal," of a four-point scale presented to the respondent. When we examine the percentages who "agree a great deal" or the complete distribution taking into account the two intermediate categories, the conclusion is unchanged.

26. The question presented the respondent with a four-point scale anchored at the ends by "most of the time" and "hardly at all." We have only shown in the table the percentages falling in the category "most of the time," but the finding remained unchanged when we examine the other extreme "hardly at all" or the total distribution of scores.

27. The reader must transport himself back to the era of the 1950s when a television set was still costly and not universal in American households. Poor households could afford it less and, as the evidence shows, got it later. See Bogart, (1958: 11-17) which also documents that small households, especially those without children, were the last to acquire television. The annual income of old widows, abysmally low in the 1950s (the median shown in table 3.1 was $1,285) would have been likely to deprive them of a set and handicap them greatly in the comparison of television viewing. The effect of widowhood may be real, but the link in the process may have been economic rather than motivational. By the 1970s, however, television had become cheap and almost universal. Whether they could afford it or not, even old widows probably would no longer be handicapped in any comparison.

28. Again the reader should re-examine table 3.1 and note the very low educational attainment among the cohort of women who had grown up around the turn of the century and had become old and widowed by the 1950s. It is well established that the major and strong determinant of reading print is formal education. Thus this group would be especially handicapped in the comparison with the married. The difference in magazine reading is real but may simply reflect the educational disadvantage that preceded their widowhood. Although in the aggregate we find little difference between widowed and married in reading about the campaign in newspapers, it should also be noted that old widows did less such reading which was obscured in the overall finding. This is consistent with the magazine finding and with the argument just advanced.

29. The question presented four levels of exposure from "frequently" to "never" watching. The conclusion is the same whichever extreme category we examine.

30. No data on religious attendance are presented for the 1956 panel, although the variable was available. The code categories used in the study to score the frequency of attendance made the findings noncomparable to the 1970s findings, and because of their cruder nature yield only a loose measure of the variable. In the 1970s panel, although the measurement was far more refined, the high end of the scale was anchored at attendance "every week," and thus we cannot examine such extreme levels of social and/or spiritual involvement as was done in the NORC analysis where "more than once a week" was coded separately.

31. In the interest of precision it should be noted that the 1970s question used "a year ago" as the reference point for the judgment of changes in financial situation, whereas the 1950s questions used "the last few years."

32. One other distinctive feature of the design imposed on the panel should be noted which also makes the Michigan findings more striking than the NORC findings. The NORC sample included widows who were about to remarry at the time they were interviewed along with all the other kinds of widows in the nation. They contribute something to the results although they are a small minority of the group. By confining the present analysis to the persistently widowed, we already know at the first wave interview that none of them, whether by intent or circumstance, will remarry within the next four years. Despite that commitment or consignment to widowhood in the years ahead, negative effects at first wave are few and modest in magnitude.

33. The two NORC surveys, as the reader will recall, asked respondents whether their spouse had died and how long ago it occurred. Those results pooled over the two surveys and younger and older white widows (including those in their eighties) showed that 65 percent had been widowed more than five years. (Since widows with a history of divorce could not be screened out of the SRC sample, they were left in the NORC sample also in tabulating duration of widowhood.) The NORC finding, with appropriate adjustment, can be applied to the panel group of persistently widowed on the first wave of measurement in 1972 when both samples were equivalent in design and included all widows forty years of age or older. By the final wave of the panel four years later, the SRC widows were being restudied at a more advanced stage of life than the NORC sample was and they would have been further along in their career of widowhood. However, even when studied for the first time in 1972, the panel did differ in one essential way. Because of the exclusion of those who would later suffer attrition from death or institutionalization (mainly the very old as reported in note 5), the panel members were younger than the NORC cross-sectional sample (which did include those who would be subject to later attrition). By standardization, combining the NORC measurements of duration of widowhood at the various age

levels with proper weights, we can infer the findings that would have been obtained if the NORC widows had the same age distribution as the panel members. That standardized and reasonable estimate of duration of widowhood in 1972 is that 62 percent of the persistently widowed had been bereaved more than five years before, 12 percent within the previous year, and 26 percent more than one but not more than five years earlier.

34. In order to build up the statistical base, all the recent white widows in the sample, no matter how young or old, are included in this analysis. For comparability, all persistently widowed and married, no matter what their age, are also included in this special analysis. Thus any change in the findings for these groups from table 3.2 to 3.3 is not error, but reflects the different age boundaries. As the reader can note, the changes are negligible, indicating that being "very young" rather than "young" has almost no effect on the patterns of the widowed and married.

35. One influential body of theory in the literature and some empirical evidence suggests that widows who have had time to prepare themselves as a result of the long illness of the husband, in contrast with those widowed abruptly, experience less difficulty following the actual widowhood. This process would also reduce the likelihood of short-term negative effects revealed in the third wave. See for example. Glick, Weiss, and Parkes, (1974: especially 13−15). For evidence to the contrary, see Clayton, et al., (1973); Gerber et al., (1975). Various findings in Lopata's large and careful sample survey of Chicago widows show the severity of the situation for many during the final phase of marriage. One-sixth had a sick husband at home for a year or more during his terminal illness. (Among the remainder many of the husbands also were ill but being cared for in hospitals.) One of her widows reports: "My husband was sick for eleven years and was in bed for seven and couldn't move . . . . I had a hospital bed in the living room for seven years and I slept on the davenport" (1971: 47−59).

36. The parsimonious explanation for the lower level of television viewing among the persistently widowed, advanced in note 27, may be relevant to the behavior of the recently widowed while still married. The terminal illnesses of their husbands may have drained their money as well as their time and energy and made them less likely to buy a set in that era when it was still an expensive luxury item. The death of the husband may have released some money as well as time which, though not plentiful given the circumstances of widows, could nevertheless be used for new purposes including the purchases of a set, thus explaining in some degree the rapid rise in the viewing of the recently widowed.

4. Conclusion

1. The SRC survey of "The Quality of American Life" reports the same surprising finding, although it is based on a very small number of cases and loose controls. "It is apparent immediately that married people, both women and men, are the most content with their family life. Widowed women, however, are equally positive in their appraisals, in sharp contrast to widowed men who are considerably more negative. It is not surprising to find divorced and separated people relatively dissatisfied with their family life, but the strikingly negative reports of the men in this group were not so predictable" (Campbell, et al., 1976: 339).

2. Other subtle differences in the roles of the widower and widow and in the disruption produced by the death of the wife rather than the husband are carefully conceptualized by Berardo and help to illuminate our findings. To be sure, a widow might argue for the opposite conclusion using the same basic logic. Just as the widower might have to take on the unfamiliar assignment of homemaker-house-keeper, the widow might have to take on the assignment of breadwinner-bookkeeper for which she had no previous experience. As one of Lopata's widows said: "You have to take care of your own checks and banking and bills, and this is a problem, when you've never done this" (1971: 70). But Berardo's assertion that the widower would be less likely to receive assistance in his new plight seems well grounded, and the empirical findings are the ultimate test of the two arguments. More severe effects of widowhood or divorce on men were also doeumented in a small-scale study of the aged living in three small towns in Missouri. Scores on a general adjustment scale were the same for married and widowed or divorced women, whereas married men showed much better adjustment than widowers or divorced men. It is in the very nature of their situation that widowhood was much more recent for men than women in the Missouri study (just as it was in our nationwide samples), and the authors speculate that time to adjust may account for the differential pattern (Pihlblad and McNamara, 1965: 59−60). Also see Troll (1971: 269, 275) for some additional observations on the special difficulties of widowers.

3. This is not to suggest that sex makes no difference. Women, whether married or widowed are more frequent churchgoers than men, a pattern that has been documented in many surveys in the United States and other countries.

4. As the reader will recall, the objective question on history of hospitalization or disability was

asked in only the 1978 and 1980 NORC surveys. The pooled size of the groups of widowed and divorced or separated older men over all the surveys is small enough, and shrinks to almost nothing with only two surveys. The shaky findings were omitted from the text and the table, but they are too dramatic to be ignored, and are much higher than for the corresponding groups of women. 62 percent of the divorced or separated and 32 percent of the widowers report being hospitalized or disabled within two or more of the last five years. The contrasted finding among older married men, 14 percent, is the same as that for the older married women reported in table 2.2. The findings by Helsing, et al., (1981) reported in chapter 1 of significantly higher mortality rates for widowers, age fifty-five to sixty-four or sixty-five to seventy-four at the time of bereavement than for married men of the same age parallel our finding of differential morbidity. Greater morbidity in a group of old widowers matched in important respects with a group of widows is also documented in Irwin Gerber, et al., (1975).

5. The reduced mortality found among widowers who have remarried has led to the speculation that the healthy ones decide to remarry, leaving behind the sicker ones whose prospects are poorer. If so, this would change the argument in our text as to the direction of the bias among the surviving widowers surveyed. A refined analysis by Helsing, et al., (1981) counters the speculation. Among widowers who survived for three years—all relatively healthy at the time of bereavement—those who remarried within that period were found to have a lower mortality rate (computed over the subsequent nine years) than those who had not remarried within the first three years. It is remarriage that insures them, not an initial factor of especially good health. And it is life as a widower that progressively produces the death toll rather than initially poor health—underscoring the basic finding of our study of widowers.

6. Long ago, Durkheim echoed the same theme—though in a more somber tone. His comparisons of suicide rates among married, widowed, and divorced men and women revealed that "divorced persons of both sexes kill themselves between three and four times as often as married persons, although younger . . . and considerably more often than widowed persons in spite of the aggravation resulting for the latter from their advanced age. He then mentions "the exceptional tendency to suicide shown by divorced *men*" (italics supplied). His replicated data for Saxony, for example, showed a rate for divorced women about two-and-a-half times greater than for married women, whereas among divorced men the rate more than quadruples (1951: 262, 273).

Bibliography

Anderson, Charles. 1949. "Aspects of Pathological Grief and Mourning." *International Journal of Psychoanalysis* 30: 48–55.

Benney, Mark; Riesman, David; and Star, Shirley. 1956. "Age and Sex in the Interview." *American Journal of Sociology* 62: 143–52.

Berardo, Felix M. 1967. "Social Adaptation to Widowhood Among a Rural–Urban Aged Population." *Washington Agricultural Experiment Station Bulletin 689*. College of Agriculture, Washington State University.

———. 1968. "Widowhood Status in the United States: Perspective on a Neglected Aspect of the Family Life-cycle." *Family Coordinator* 17: 191–203.

———. 1970. "Survivorship and Social Isolation: The Case of the Aged Widower." *Family Coordinator* 19: 11–25.

Blalock, Hubert M. 1970. "Estimating Measurement Error Using Multiple Indicators and Several Points in Time." *American Sociological Review* 35: 101–11.

Bogart, Leo. 1968. *The Age of Television*, Second Edition. New York: Ungar.

Bradburn, Norman. 1969. *The Structure of Psychological Well-Being*. Chicago: Aldine.

Bradburn, Norman, and Caplovitz, David. 1965. *Reports on Happiness*. Chicago: Aldine.

Campbell, Angus; Converse, Philip; Miller, Warren; and Stokes, Donald. 1966. *Elections and The Political Order*. New York: Wiley.

Campbell, Angus; Converse, Philip; and Rodgers, Willard. 1976. *The Quality of American Life*. New York: Russell Sage Foundation.

Carp, Frances. 1976. "Housing and Living Environments of Older People." In *Handbook of Aging and the Social Sciences*, pp. 244–71. Edited by Robert Binstock and Ethel Shanas. New York: Van Nostrand.

Carter, Hugh, and Glick, Paul. 1976. *Marriage and Divorce: A Social Economic Study*, Revised Edition. Cambridge: Harvard University Press.

Chevan, Albert, and Korson, J. Henry. 1972. "The Widowed Who Live Alone: An Examination of Social and Demographic Factors." *Social Forces* 51: 45–53.

Clayton, Paula. 1973. "The Clinical Morbidity of the First Year of Bereavement: A Review." *Comprehensive Psychiatry* 14: 151–57.

Clayton, Paula; Halikas, James; and Maurice, William. 1972. "The Depression of Widowhood." *British Journal of Psychiatry* 120: 71–78.

Converse, Philip; Cutler, Stephen; Glenn, Norval; and Hyman, Herbert. 1978. "The General Social Surveys." *Contemporary Sociology* 7: 532–49.

Cosneck, Bernard. 1970. "Family Patterns of Older Widowed Jewish People." *Family Coordinator* 19: 371–72.

Cutler, Neal. 1978. "The Social Dynamics of Subjective Age Identification Among Older Women." Paper delivered at the Eleventh International Congress of Gerontology. Tokyo, August.

Danto, Bruce. 1975. "Bereavement and the Widows of Slain Police Officers." In *Bereavement: Its Psychosocial Aspects*, pp. 150–63. Edited by Bernard Schoenberg, et al. New York: Columbia University Press.

DeMaio, Theresa, 1980. "Refusals: Who, Where and Why." *Public Opinion Quarterly* 44: 223–33.

Durkheim, Emile. 1951. *Suicide*. New York: Macmillan-Free Press.

Ferraro, Kenneth. 1980. "Self-Ratings of Health Among the Old and the Old-Old." *Journal of Health and Social Behavior* 21: 377–83.

Freud, Sigmund. 1942. *Beyond the Pleasure Principle*, Second Edition. London: Hogarth Press.

Gerber, Irwin; Rusalem, Roslyn; Hannon, Natalie; Battin, Delia; and Arkin, Arthur. 1975. "Anticipatory Grief and Aged Widows and Widowers." *Journal of Gerontology* 30: 225–29.

Glenn, Norval. 1975. "The Contribution of Marriage to the Psychological Well-Being of Males and Females." *Journal of Marriage and the Family* 37: 549–99.

Glick, Ira; Weiss, Robert; and Parkes, C. Murray. 1974. *The First Year of Bereavement*. New York: John Wiley.

Harvey, Carol D., and Bahr, Howard. 1974. "Widowhood, Morale, and Affiliation." *Journal of Marriage and the Family* 36: 97–106.

Heise, David E. 1970. "Comment on 'The Estimation of Measurement Error in Panel Data'." *American Sociological Review* 35: 117.

Helsing, Knud; Szklo, Moyses; and Comstock, George. 1981. "Factors Associated with Mortality after Widowhood." *American Journal of Public Health* 71: 802–9.

Hyman, Herbert; Cobb, William; Feldman, Jacob; Hart Clyde; and Stember, Charles. 1954. *Interviewing in Social Research*. Chicago: University of Chicago Press.

Hyman, Herbert; Wright, Charles; and Hopkins, Terence. 1962. *Applications of Methods of Evaluation*. Berkeley: University of California Press.

Hyman, Herbert. 1972. *Secondary Analysis of Sample Surveys*. New York: Wiley.

Inter-university Consortium for Political Research. 1979. *The SRC American Panel Study: 1956, 1958, 1960; The American National Election Series: 1972, 1974, and 1976*, 5 vols. Ann Arbor: Institute for Social Research, University of Michigan.

Kendall, Patricia. 1954. *Conflict and Mood: Factors Affecting Stability of Response*. New York: Free Press.

Kitagawa, Evelyn, and Hauser, Philip. 1973. *Differential Mortality in the United States: A Study in Socio-Economic Epidemiology*. Cambridge: Harvard University Press.

Kivett, Vira. 1978. "Loneliness and the Rural Widow." *Family Coordinator* 27: 389–94.

Kraus, Arthur, and Lilienfeld, Abraham. 1959. "Some Epidemiological Aspects of the High Mortality in the Young Widowed Group." *Journal of Chronic Diseases* 10: 207–17.

Kutner, Bernard; Fanshel, David; Togo, Alice; and Langner, Thomas. 1960. *Five Hundred Over Sixty: A Community Survey on Aging*. New York: Russell Sage Foundation.

Lopata, Helena. 1973. *Widowhood in an American City*. Cambridge: Schenkman.

———. 1975. "On Widowhood: Grief Work and Identity Reconstruction." *Journal of Geriatric Psychiatry* 31: 41–55.

———. 1979. *Women as Widows: Support Systems*. New York: Elsevier.

Maddison, David, and Viola, Agnes. 1968. "The Health of Widows in the Year Following Bereavement." *Journal of Psychosomatic Research* 12: 297–306.

Mallan, Lucy. 1975. "Young Widows and Their Children: A Comparative Report." *Social Security Bulletin*. May.

"Marriage is Good for Health and Longevity, Studies Say." 1979. *New York Times*. May 8, p. C–1.

Marris, Peter. 1958. *Widows and Their Families*. London: Routledge and Kegan Paul.

Miller, Warren; Miller, Arthur; and Schneider, Edward. 1980. *American National Election*

Studies Data Sourcebook, 1952–1978. Cambridge: Harvard University Press.

National Council on the Aging. 1975. *The Myth and Reality of Aging in America.* Washington, D.C.

———. 1981. *Aging in the 80s: America in Transition.* Washington, D.C.

National Opinion Research Center, 1978. *General Social Surveys, 1972–1978.* University of Chicago.

Parkes, C. Murray. 1964. "The Effects of Bereavement on Physical and Mental Health,- Study of the Medical Records of Widows." *British Medical Journal* 2: 274–79.

———. 1965. "Bereavement and mental illness, Part I: A clinical study of the grief of bereaved psychiatric patients. Part II: A Classification of bereavement reactions." *British Journal of Medical Psychology* 38: 1–26.

———. 1970. "The First Year of Bereavement: A Longitudinal Study of the Reaction of London Widows to the Death of Their Husbands." *Psychiatry* 33: 444–67.

———. 1972. *Bereavement: Studies of Grief in Adult Life.* New York: International University Press.

———. 1975. "Unexpected and Untimely Bereavement: A Statistical Study of Young Boston Widows and Widowers." In *Bereavement: Its Psychosocial Aspects,* pp 119–38. Edited by Bernard Schoenberg, Irwin Gerber, Alfred Wiener, Austin Kutscher, David Peretz, and Arthur Carr. New York: Columbia University Press.

Pihlblad, Terence, and McNamara, Robert. 1965. "Social Adjustment of Elderly People in Three Small Towns." In *Older People and Their Social World,* pp 59–60. Edited by Arnold Rose and Warren Peterson. Philadelphia: F. A. Davis Company.

Pihlblad, Terence, and Adams, David. 1972. "Widowhood, Social Participation and Life Satisfaction." *Aging and Human Development* 3: 323–30.

Pope, Hallowell, and Mueller, Charles W. 1976. "The Intergenerational Transmission of Marital Instability: Comparisons by Race and Sex." *Journal of Social Issues* 32: 46–65.

Robinson, John; and Shaver, Philip. 1969. *Measures of Social Psychological Attitudes.* Ann Arbor: Institute for Social Research, University of Michigan.

Rosenberg, Morris. 1962. "Test Factor Standardization as a Method of Interpretation." *Social Forces* 41: 53–61.

Schaeffer, Nora. 1980. "Evaluating Race of Interviewer Effects in a National Survey." *Sociological Methods and Research* 8: 400–19.

Schuman, Howard, and Converse, Jean. 1971. "The Effects of Black and White Interviewers on Black Responses in 1968." *Public Opinion Quarterly* 35: 44–68.

Shanas, Ethel. 1959. "Some Sociological Research Findings about Older People Pertinent to Social Work." In *Toward Better Understanding of the Aging.* Vol. 1. New York: Council on Social Work Education. pp 1–10.

Shanas, Ethel; Townsend, Peter; Wedderburn, Dorothy; Friis, Henning; Milhoj, Pool; and Stehouwer, Jan. 1968. *Old People in Three Industrial Societies.* New York: Atherton Press.

Smith, Tom, and Stephenson, Bruce. 1979. *An Analysis of Test/Retest Experiments on the 1972, 1973, 1974, and 1978 General Social Surveys.* Chicago: National Opinion Research Center, GSS Technical Report No. 14.

Social Security Administration. 1980. "Preliminary Findings from the 1978 Survey of Survivor Families with Children." *Research and Statistics Note* No. 12, Nov. 7.

Spreitzer, Elmer, and Snyder, Eldon. 1974. "Correlates of Life Satisfaction Among the Aged." *Journal of Gerontology* 29: 454–58.

Sumner, William Graham. 1913. *Folkways.* Boston: Ginn & Co.

Thompson, Gayle. 1980. "Economic Status of Late Middle-Aged Widows." In *Transitions of Aging*, pp. 133–49. Edited by Nancy Datan and Nancy Lohmann. New York: Academic Press.

Townsend, Peter. 1957. *The Family Life of Old People: An Inquiry in East London*. New York: Free Press.

Troll, Lillian E. 1971. "The Family of Later Life: A Decade Review." *Journal of Marriage and the Family* 33: 263–90.

United States of America. Census Bureau. "Marital Status and Family Status: March 1970." 1971. Current Population Reports. Series P–20, No. 212, March.

———. ———. "Marital Status and Living Arrangements: March 1974." 1974. Current Population Reports. Series P–20, No. 271, October.

———. Department of Health, Education, and Welfare. "Final Marriage Statistics, 1974." 1976. Monthly Vital Statistics Reports. Vol. 25, No. 2, Supplement, May 5.

Wright, Charles R. 1975. "Social Structure and Mass Communications Behavior." In *The Idea of Social Structure: Papers in Honor of Robert K. Merton* pp. 379–413. Edited by Lewis Coser. New York: Harcourt Brace Jovanovich.

Wiley, David E., and Wiley, James A. 1970. "The Estimation of Measurement Error in Panel Data." *American Sociological Review*. 35: 112–17.

Wretmark, Gerdt. 1959. "A Study in Grief Reactions." *Acta Pschiat. Neurol. Scand.* Supplement 136, pp. 292–99.

Index

Herbert H. Hyman is Crowell University Professor of the Social Sciences and former chairman of the Department of Sociology, Wesleyan University. He has been Professor of Sociology at the Graduate Division of Columbia University, chairman of that department, and an Associate Director of Columbia's Bureau of Applied Social Research. His books include *Survey Design and Analysis, Interviewing in Social Research, Political Socialization,* and *Secondary Analysis of Sample Surveys.* He is coauthor of *Readings in Reference Group Theory, The Enduring Effects of Education,* and *Education's Lasting Influence on Values.*